The Writing Book

The Writing Book

How to develop
young writers

Zoë and Timothy Paramour

BLOOMSBURY EDUCATION
LONDON OXFORD NEW YORK NEW DELHI SYDNEY

BLOOMSBURY EDUCATION
Bloomsbury Publishing Plc
50 Bedford Square, London, WC1B 3DP, UK
29 Earlsfort Terrace, Dublin 2, Ireland

BLOOMSBURY, BLOOMSBURY EDUCATION and the Diana logo are trademarks of
Bloomsbury Publishing Plc

First published in Great Britain, 2023

A catalogue record for this book is available from the British Library

ISBN: PB: 978-1-8019-9145-2; ePDF: 978-1-8019-9143-8; ePub: 978-1-8019-9144-5

2 4 6 8 10 9 7 5 3 1 (paperback)

Typeset by Newgen KnowledgeWorks Pvt. Ltd., Chennai, India
Printed and bound in India by Replika Press Pvt. Ltd

MIX
Paper from
responsible sources
FSC® C016779

To find out more about our authors and books visit www.bloomsbury.com
and sign up for our newsletters

We'd like to dedicate this book to all of our pupils,
past and present.

Contents

Acknowledgements

In the words of Lisa Simpson (2011), 'Writing is the hardest thing ever!' The process of writing this book was made easier with the help of the following:

- Hannah Marston – for believing in this book and encouraging us from the very start
- Emily Badger – for her feedback and support, and for going through our manuscript with a fine-tooth comb to turn it into the book you're currently holding
- Deliveroo – for bringing us iced, caffeinated beverages during the long days of writing in the heatwave
- the fan we bought from Wilko
- the iMac repair man who recovered the first three chapters when our computer crashed
- each other (aw).

Introduction

In December 2017, an Indonesian archaeologist named Basran Burhan embarked on a daring trek across the island of Sulawesi, traversing mountains and thick forest paths to reach the mouth of a limestone cave, only accessible during the tropical dry season. Inside the cave, he made a remarkable discovery: a painting of a wild pig, daubed on the cave wall some 45,000 years ago. It is believed to be the oldest piece of representational art ever discovered. Since the dawn of humanity, our species has been driven by an insatiable urge to make our mark – to leave an imprint that says, if nothing else, 'I was here'. It is one of the key distinctions between us and other animals, at least as far as we know; it's possible that our cats are secret playwrights, but we've seen no evidence of it!

The first true civilisations are believed to have emerged in Mesopotamia's fertile crescent, between the banks of the Rivers Tigris and Euphrates, around seven thousand years ago. The Mesopotamians started to do something more sophisticated than drawing mere images of objects: they began to combine particular pictures in uniform ways to carve detailed messages in stone. These evolved into Egyptian hieroglyphics and the beginnings of what we might call writing. The next great innovation came from the Phoenicians, a powerful trading culture during the first millennium BCE, who developed written symbols that weren't recognisable pictures at all, but merely stood for particular sounds. The Phoenician system of writing was exported to Europe, where it was picked up by the Ancient Greeks, who named the first two letters alpha and beta; thus the *alphabeta*, or alphabet, was born. The rest, as they say, is history – quite literally, as it was the development of writing that enabled human beings to record our own history in the first place. It was writing that enabled scholars to share their discoveries and governments to administer their kingdoms. From papyrus to parchment to paper, from the monastic scribe to the printing press and the word processor, it is writing, more than any other human invention, that has built the civilisation in which we live. Writing is, quite simply, one of the most important things that there is…

But try telling some of your pupils that.

Why this book is needed

Learning to write is hard and learning to write well is even harder. Implausible though it may seem, some of the young people in your class may not be entirely grateful to the Mesopotamians and the Phoenicians for breathing life into the written word. They can speak, after all, and make themselves understood. They've got spell-checkers and autocorrect on all their devices (take that, Phoenicians) and, for the most part, they can read written English well enough to function comfortably in everyday life. What more do they need to know about writing?

Well, quite a lot, actually. The ability to write persuasively is hugely empowering, for example, and the ability to entertain others with one's writing is tremendously fulfilling. The problem, as with so many things, is that many of the advantages that come with *being good at writing* are only apparent once you get there. Teaching children to write is not entirely different to coaxing them up a hill or mountain: it's painstaking for both of you, they're likely to moan the whole way up and sometimes you're not actually sure that you're going the right way. But then you get to the top and you show them the view. You can see the wonder in their eyes and the sharp intake of breath before they shrug self-consciously and say: 'Yeah, it's alright I suppose.' But the wonder was real – and you both know it. That's what teaching is all about, right?

It can be tempting to think that all our pupils must, eventually, learn to write through osmosis – that if we simply expose them to enough examples of competent writing, they will learn to pick up the tricks of the trade without effort. It can be tempting to treat writing as an inherently creative, personal and subjective exercise, but this is not always the case. There is a methodology to it and this sometimes needs to be taught explicitly. This is especially true for children who may not speak English at home. This book is intended to support teachers by taking decent emerging writers and making them truly proficient. However, regardless of where your pupils are on this journey, the same principles apply: they need lots of good examples, plenty of opportunities to practise and specific, targeted feedback.

So how do we get our pupils to the summit of the hill? How do we genuinely and meaningfully improve their writing? How do we get them writing sentences that *sound good*? How do we get them writing whole texts that someone might genuinely want to read? Well, like any steep climb, it isn't easy but it's also not impossible.

Unfortunately, generations of teachers have been let down by a lot of very questionable guidance and advice. The National Curriculum never really gets it right, whoever is in government, and Key Stage 2 assessments rarely incentivise the right things. Some people will tell you that if we could just find the right checklist of magic ingredients that children must include in their writing, then we'll finally nail it. These self-appointed experts would have you take up half the space in your children's English books with detailed lists of objectives and success criteria like *use powerful adjectives* and *use personification to describe a setting*. At the other extreme, a different but equally questionable group of experts will tell you that if we stop telling children how to write completely and just let them '*embrace their creativity*', then all sorts of wonderful things will happen by magic. For these irrepressible free spirits, your job as a teacher is merely to inspire your pupils – to give them something that they'll want to write about.

Instinctively, most practising teachers know that neither of these groups of experts has got it quite right.

This book outlines what you might call our philosophy when it comes to the teaching of writing, if that doesn't sound too pretentious. That philosophy can be summed up by saying that *writing is there to be read*. That seems obvious but it's a principle too often missing from the way that we are encouraged to approach the teaching of writing. The problem with both the 'exhaustive list of success criteria' approach and the 'just let them be creative, dude' approach is that both ignore the role of the reader. The first approach suggests that the writer's role is to take orders *from* some established source of knowledge about what makes good writing, rather than creating something *for* an audience. The second approach encourages a sort of creative narcissism on the part of the writer, by which nothing matters other than their own desire for self-expression, regardless of whether or not it resonates with anyone else. To really enhance our pupils' writing, we need a realistic, practical path that places the reader at the centre of everything.

We do not claim to be experts on anything, apart from, perhaps, the various tracks and characters on Mario Kart™ 8. We have attempted to incorporate some of what is known about the way in which the reader's mind works into these pages, including some of the insights from Jane Yellowlees-Douglas's excellent book *The Reader's Brain* (2015). However, we are ordinary teachers, just like you, and we have distilled our experiences and discoveries into the book that you're holding. The words on these pages are informed by both triumph and disaster in the classroom, and we offer them in all humility, to guide you through all the unconvincing noise that's out there about the way we teach writing in schools.

Who are we?

We are both experienced teachers. We met while working at the same school in North London in 2010, we got married in 2016 and we are both now senior leaders at different schools. We live in Enfield with our two cats and, when we're not teaching, we write about teaching. Our marriage survived the effort of writing *The Grammar Book* in 2020 and now we thought we'd put it to the test again. After all, what are summer holidays for if not painstakingly compiling an entire book about the job you do for the rest of the year?!

We love our fellow teachers. Most of our friends and quite a few of our relatives are teachers. Our profession is full of wonderful, intelligent people who, despite having the qualifications to do something far easier for far more money, chose instead to do something truly important and noble. It's often a very thankless job and, all too often, teachers are allowed to feel that they aren't doing it well enough. If these books have one purpose, it is to offer practical support and reassurance to our professional brothers and sisters, wherever you are and whatever challenges you currently face.

The story so far

Teaching writing in schools can be a frustrating business. It feels like the sands are constantly shifting beneath our feet. If you've been teaching for a while, you probably feel exhausted from the constant churn of new initiatives and frameworks that have come along over the past couple of decades. If you're new to the profession, you might feel bewildered by the expectations set out by the Department for Education (DfE) and the National Curriculum. Different governments have tried in different ways to quantify and measure what we mean by 'good writing'. Most teachers probably feel that these attempts have largely failed.

At the start of the twenty-first century, the National Literacy Strategy (NLS) was in use in most English primary schools. This was a detailed and very prescriptive framework that outlined what should be covered and when during children's English lessons, to the extent that the number of minutes allocated to different activities was specified on a diagram of a clock that will still haunt your dreams if you were teaching back then. In fairness to the NLS, there is good evidence that it did raise standards, especially for children from the lowest starting points, but not always as quickly or as easily as it could have. The NLS was accompanied by the Key Stage 2 Writing Test, in which children were assessed on two writing tasks (a longer and a shorter one), according to a mark scheme that sought to outline an objective-scoring framework. The problem, as anyone who ever tried to use those mark schemes will recall, was that they simply weren't objective. However many categories you broke the scores down into (up to two marks for sentence structure, up to three marks for organisation and layout, etc.), the actual allocation of marks was always subjective. That is to say, the examiner could only assess the effect that the writing had on *them*. Moderation exercises in schools would routinely highlight the wildly different marks that two different markers might give to the same pieces of work.

As the NLS was scaled back and then, by 2009, discontinued altogether, a new approach to assessing children's writing became fashionable: Assessing Pupil Progress (APP) grids. These had quite evidently been dreamed up by people who had been far too long out of the classroom and made teachers' lives a misery. They attempted to itemise every feature or element that you might want or expect to see in a child's writing and highlight them on a massive table whenever the child deployed that feature or element. Again, it was supposed to be fair and objective, but it caused utter confusion. Some schools would use the grids to assess individual pieces of work while some would use them as rolling records of achievement for children over an extended period of time. Some teachers would accept work done with extensive adult support as evidence to support APP judgements, while others would not. It was an utterly subjective, massively onerous, needlessly bureaucratic mess of an educational initiative. And then things got worse. Michael Gove showed up.

In 2010, the coalition government came to power, promising, as all incoming governments do, to address inadequate standards in English children's literacy skills. Their solution was traditional rigour: teach them grammar like they did in the good old days! However, their priority was teaching grammar in such a way that it could easily be tested. The problem is that grammar is debatable and contestable, full of grey areas and exceptions. The DfE found themselves inventing arbitrary grammatical definitions and distinctions that had no basis in linguistic scholarship, just so that they could be tested. Politicians found themselves embarrassing themselves on TV by giving perfectly acceptable answers to test questions, which, according to their own mark schemes, were wrong.

Now we have a framework for assessing writing in Key Stage 2 that, as always, is more subjective than anyone is willing to admit, and which incentivises an almost entirely arbitrary array of linguistic devices that happen to be fashionable at the moment. How is anyone supposed to navigate these maddening currents of top-down political change? We believe that the trick is to step back and stop worrying about what the government is saying today, because by tomorrow they'll have changed their minds anyway. Our job as teachers is to make our pupils into good writers, not to second guess the whims of politicians and civil service policy advisors. We are better placed than any of them to give our pupils what they need.

The important thing, therefore, is not what politicians and their advisors think good writing is. They don't know, they never have and they probably never will. What matters is whether we know, as teachers, what good writing is. If we do, we can pass that onto our pupils and then, whatever daft expectations get dreamed up by the DfE, the children we teach will have a fighting chance of rising to meet them.

How to use this book

You may wish to use this book entirely as a reference resource, dipping into the chapters that you need as you need them. However, we have aimed to make it rewarding and worthwhile for those who join us for the whole journey.

Each chapter in this book focuses on a different aspect of writing. You will notice fairly quickly that it has not been divided up by text type or genre. There isn't a section on 'how to teach play scripts' and a section on 'how to teach non-chronological reports'. It's perfectly reasonable to ask children to apply different features to different types of text, but we're not convinced that it gets us any closer to the essence of 'good writing'.

There is also very little on stimuli for writing or how to inspire your pupils. That's partly because there are tons of books on the subject out there already, but it's also because (and this is going to be controversial) inspiring children, at least for the time it takes to complete a short piece of writing, isn't actually that hard. As experienced teachers, you know your pupils and you know what will motivate and enthuse them. We'd bet that *that* isn't the bit you find difficult. There are plenty of self-appointed experts out there who will tell you that 'anyone can teach grammar, but the real skill is being able to fire your pupils' imagination!' Doesn't that sound lovely? Doesn't it just make you feel warm and fuzzy inside? Well, that's fine, except for the fact that it's completely untrue and we all know it. We can spend all day firing our pupils' imaginations but, in the end, there is no substitute for the subject knowledge that we need to help our pupils to use their imaginations effectively.

At this point, you may be feeling your first flush of apprehension. What have you got yourself into? Is this book going to be a dry lecture on technical linguistic terminology? The answer is a resounding 'no'. This is a book about how to let your pupils' imaginations take flight and how to help them express their ideas in glorious technicolour. However, we promised to be honest with you and we intend to keep that promise. If you are serious about developing your pupils' writing skills, you need to think seriously, and deeply, about how language works. The good news is that we will guide you through all the technical stuff. We are here to help, we promise!

This is not a book about grammar – that was our last one – but, inevitably, it does *use* grammatical terminology quite a lot. Wherever we refer to any of that pesky grammatical vocabulary that we ourselves were never taught in school, we include a brief explanation. However, if you want to find out more about a particular topic as we go, we have also included page references from *The Grammar Book*. If you're not hugely confident about your subject knowledge when it comes to grammar, you might find it helpful to use both books in conjunction with one another.

Our aim throughout this book is to unravel the mystery of writing. It is not a book about inspiring children to write or about identifying the features of different genres. It is about how to write, and how to make your writing *sound good*.

What will I find in each section?

Part One, *The power of writing*, comprises three chapters and sets out our stall, so to speak. There are three fundamental principles that we will keep coming back to throughout the book and, to start with, we examine each one in detail. The first chapter is about awareness of one's reader which, as we have already said, lies at the heart of good writing. The second chapter is about the crafting of individual sentences – a skill that lies at the heart of the writing process but sometimes seems so mysterious as to be beyond the reach of discrete teaching input. The third chapter is about succinctness, and it explores the importance of efficient language choices.

Part Two, *Selecting words and arranging your writing*, explores the various challenges that our pupils face when selecting the right language to use. It covers topics such as descriptive language, direct and reported speech, different registers and tones, and the techniques that a writer can use to elicit specific emotional responses from their reader.

Part Three, *Writing it down*, explores the processes involved in writing: drafting, planning and editing, making the writing *flow*, and coming up with a beginning and an ending. It is about how our pupils can actually get their thoughts down on the page.

Every chapter is about a different theme and each one contains the same three sections. We start with **Why it matters**, outlining what the chapter is about and why we think that particular theme is important. Then we move on to the **How to do it** section, exploring and addressing the challenges that a teacher faces when teaching that particular theme, with practical advice. Each chapter has a **Summary** of the key points and a **Where next?** section that highlights what is coming up in the next chapter. The very final section in each chapter is called **Resources and modelled texts**, which contains materials and examples that you can lift from the book and use in the classroom. Copies of these resources are also available to download from the Bloomsbury Education website. When you see this logo, it means that the resources are available to download from bloomsbury.pub/the-writing-book.

We hope that this book will be useful and enjoyable for you, and that it will empower you to improve your pupils' writing. When you're ready, let's dive into Part One.

The power of writing

Chapter 1

Dear reader: Writing for an audience

In the 1993 film *Shadowlands*, the character of C.S. Lewis, played by Anthony Hopkins, says: 'We read to know we are not alone.' This wonderful line encapsulates all three of the fundamental principles of this book: it is a simple but elegantly crafted sentence, it is gloriously succinct and, most importantly for the purposes of this chapter, it eloquently expresses the bond between reader and writer.

The magic of the written word is hard to overstate. By placing the little squiggles and patterns that we call letters on this page in this particular configuration, we, the writers, are able to reach out to you, our reader, across space and time and share our thoughts. We can't see you and you can't see us. For all we know, you may even be reading this after our deaths, although that would either mean that this book was more successful than we expected or that our next plane flight was considerably less successful than we expected. We have probably never met and perhaps never will. Yet here we are – doing this together. You, dear reader, are not alone. A writer's job is to conjure that magic – to create a mental space in which they and their reader can briefly co-exist. Writing is an act of communication, or it is nothing. There is only one useful measure of how good a piece of writing is: the effect that it has on the reader – how it *sounds*.

In this book, we will often refer to the way in which a piece of writing *sounds*. This is the best verb that we have to describe *what it feels like* to read a particular word, sentence or text. In reality, of course, a passage that we read to ourselves doesn't sound like anything. We could use a different verb – *feels*, for example, or *reads*. *Tastes* would actually be quite fitting if we wanted to be even more metaphorical. However, on balance, we felt it best to stick with *sounds*.

Why it matters

Often, you will hear certain individuals, believing themselves to be so very clever, make sniffy remarks about popular fiction. Whether it's *Harry Potter*, *The Da Vinci Code* or even *Fifty Shades of Grey*, every few years a book comes along that makes these people say things like: 'The thing is, it's not actually *very good writing*.' The rest of us, not wishing to appear uncultured or stupid, might nod sagely and say something like, 'No, it's not exactly Jane Austen, is it?', even though we've never actually read anything by Jane Austen and even though, earlier in the day, we took an online quiz that confirmed that the Sorting Hat would put us in Hufflepuff. It is perfectly reasonable to suggest that a particular book has been overhyped, or that there are other books that its readers might have enjoyed even more if only they'd heard about them, but it is clearly not fair to dismiss as 'bad writing' a book that millions of people find gripping and enjoyable. Remarks like this carry an unpleasant air of snobbery and jealousy.

So, we are putting forward a very simple definition of 'good writing':

Good writing is writing that has the desired effect on the reader.

If the purpose of the writing is to entertain, and the reader is entertained, then the writing is good. If the purpose of the writing is to inform, and the reader quickly and easily gains the knowledge that they need from it, then it is good writing. If the purpose of the writing is to make a middle-ranking sales assistant feel miserable and secure a refund on a recent purchase for Karen from Northampton, and it succeeds on both counts, then the writing is good, even if Karen from Northampton is not.

To accept this definition of good writing is, on one level, to set yourself and your pupils free. No longer can a particular piece of writing be torn to shreds simply because the vocabulary is insufficiently grandiloquent *or* because its sentences are too simple *or* because it lacks certain genre-specific features. However, it does create a new conundrum: how can a writer determine the effect that their words will have on their reader? Well now, at least, we're asking the right question.

How to do it

Who are you trying to impress?

Look at this sentence:

The feline positioned itself in a sedentary position on the unfitted floor covering.

As you have probably noticed, this is essentially equivalent in meaning to 'the cat sat on the mat'. According to our definition of good writing, it is also not as good a sentence as 'the cat sat on the mat'. Why not? Because, despite the impressive vocabulary on display, this sentence is *harder to read* than its simpler counterpart. The writer is making the reader's life harder, just so they can demonstrate their own lexical brilliance. In short, they are *showing off*. That isn't appealing. In fact, for the reader, it feels condescending and alienating. Precise vocabulary is incredibly useful when it encapsulates a complex idea very simply and makes your writing easier to read. However, there is no way of communicating the idea that 'the cat sat on the mat' that makes it any clearer or more straightforward. Producing a sentence like the one above is the writer's equivalent of going on a date and spending the whole time boasting about yourself, without ever taking an interest in the person whom you're with.

You may be feeling a little uneasy at this point. Surely, you might think, you *need* your pupils to be showcasing everything that they know when they write? This is a tempting assumption, and it's probably one that we have all held at some point. However, the benefits of abandoning this way of thinking are enormous. If you can genuinely show your pupils how to communicate with their reader as clearly and as simply as possible, they won't just use sophisticated vocabulary and complex sentence structures for the sake of it – they'll use them *effectively*. The difference is enormous, and most readers can smell it a mile off.

Writing for reading

An intriguing consequence of our definition of good writing (writing that has the desired effect on the reader) is that the teaching of writing becomes inextricably linked to the teaching of empathy. The entire process of writing becomes an exercise in placing oneself in the shoes of another. This, more than anything, is why a writer must first be a reader. As teachers, we all know that our most avid readers are usually our most competent and capable writers. Just as a good cook needs to know how different flavours *taste*, on their own and in combination, a good writer needs to know how different words and phrases *sound*, on their own and in combination. So, your first job is always to get your pupils reading. You also need them to think about what they are reading, and to reflect on the impact of the language choices that an author makes. Throughout this book, you will find countless pieces of short, modelled writing that you can give to your pupils and, at the end of this chapter, you will find a list of questions that you can give them to answer about anything that they have read. Empathy with the reader must start with being a reader and with *thinking about* being a reader.

Another fairly significant consequence of focusing entirely on the reader is that your pupils need to *have* a reader in the first place. You will read their work, of course, but they should also learn to write in such a way that they have a meaningful impact on one another. This means that you need to make time in your lessons for children to read each other's work. Again, you might want to use the list of questions at the end of this chapter to scaffold the feedback that they give to one another. Even better, perhaps you can give them the opportunity to write to someone specific outside of your classroom or even beyond the school gates – to their MP or to a newspaper, for example. This gives them the chance to consider how different people might have different responses to their writing. All of this requires that your pupils have time to *edit* their writing. This is absolutely fundamental. A cook might taste a spoonful of a sauce and determine that it needs more or less of a particular ingredient. In the same way, your pupils need time to sample and revisit their own writing, and decide what is missing. This is not necessarily something that they will do instinctively. The next chapter (Macro, micro and middle: The art of the sentence) will explore some strategies for helping them to develop this habit.

Genres and text types

In the introduction, we cautioned against looking at the teaching of writing through the lens of genre and text type. This is because we think it encourages the wrong things and leads our pupils to the wrong conclusions. Let's take persuasive writing as an example. If we 'teach persuasive writing' as a unit of work, we might look at the 'features of persuasive writing' and encourage pupils to 'include these features' in their work. The result might be that their writing is full of rhetorical questions or bizarre, overblown phrases like 'only a fool would disagree with me about this!' If you're awkwardly shuffling your feet and thinking, 'Yeah…

what's wrong with that?', then let us ask you a simple question: how persuaded would *you* be by a piece of writing like that? Let's imagine that your headteacher sent you the following email:

> **Dear ...,**
>
> **I think it is quite obvious that you need a pay cut, don't you? My first reason for saying this is that we need to save money at the moment. Only a complete idiot would fail to see the need to cut back. Do you want the school to run out of money completely? My second reason for saying this is that we need to buy more playground equipment. Do you want the children to be bored at lunchtime? In conclusion, I think you need a pay cut. I'm sure you will see that I am right.**
>
> **Yours sincerely,**
>
> **The Headteacher**

We included all the best-known Key Stage 2 'features of persuasive writing', so you must be feeling pretty darn persuaded, right? Perhaps you're ready to march into school tomorrow and demand a pay cut from the head. Or, perhaps, you're not feeling remotely persuaded. More likely, you'd be utterly insulted and outraged to receive this email. Yet this is how many teachers tell children to write persuasively. Why? Well, this is complicated but also quite interesting.

We teach children to read and write simultaneously. This means that when it comes to something like persuasive writing, we are teaching our pupils to use persuasive language when they themselves need to use it, while simultaneously teaching them to defend themselves against the persuasive techniques used by those who might not have their best interests at heart, such as advertisers, politicians or malign online influencers. The latter skill is really, really important and we absolutely must give children the chance to spot and discuss persuasive language that is designed to entrap the gullible. This might start, very early on, by discussing the sort of childish techniques that our imaginary headteacher uses in his email above. So, teaching pupils about transparent rhetorical tricks is a very important part of learning to *read* persuasive writing, but that isn't necessarily what we want them to reproduce in *their own* writing. Teaching children about 'the features of persuasive writing' encourages them to think of it as a dishonest venture – a cynical set of tricks to entrap the credulous. There are two problems with this. The first problem is that it simply isn't going to work on an intelligent reader, just as you were presumably unmoved by the imaginary email from a headteacher above. The second problem, and maybe we're being astonishingly naive here, is that it's *not nice*! Without being too pious, surely we want our pupils to act with kindness and integrity? That means reframing the way in which they think about their own persuasive writing.

The 'techniques' – if you can even call them that – for honest, genuinely convincing persuasive writing are all about the person that you are trying to persuade. You need to:

- show that you understand their point of view
- recognise their goals as well as your own
- acknowledge the doubts you think they might have about whatever it is you're saying.

That's the real art of persuasion, and it's a much more edifying subject to discuss with your pupils.

It's not just persuasive writing where this principle applies. If you throw all the 'features of a non-chronological report' into a piece of writing designed to interest your reader, you'll probably create something that sounds like it was generated by a dodgy computer algorithm and bore your audience to death. If you throw all the 'features of a scary story' into a piece of fiction designed to unsettle your reader, you'll probably create a string of corny and slightly over-the-top clichés that just make them laugh.

There is no substitute for empathy. To genuinely write well, rather than producing a soulless pastiche of good writing, your pupils need to place themselves sympathetically in the shoes of their reader, and to think critically about the likely effects of their words. That's not easy but it's achievable and, once you get the hang of it, it's a lot less work for you. The good news is that there are a surprising number of tricks, techniques and short cuts that you can use to get there, and the even better news is that most of them are contained within the remaining chapters of this book.

Summary

As teachers, we can be tempted to focus on what our pupils need to *put into* their writing. Instead, we need to be asking what their reader wants to *get out* of it. This means that simple lists of 'features' to include aren't going to cut it. Instead, we need to train our pupils to look at their own writing, and the writing of others, and honestly assess its impact. There are a number of ways in which we can do this and they are the main subject of the rest of this book.

Where next?

At this point, you have two options – you can continue onto the resources and modelled text sections that are linked to this chapter or, if you're ready, you can just move onto the next chapter. In Chapter 2, we will look at the simple but complex business of crafting sentences. We will look at why some sentences feel clumsier than others, even when they are grammatically sound. We will discuss the importance of making our sentences easy to read and we will offer some practical and sometimes surprising advice to follow when writing any sentence in the English language.

Resources and modelled texts

Every chapter in this book will contain a resource section. A few of these will include practice activities or suggestions for specific tasks that you can use to teach a particular skill. However, we have also included a great deal of modelled writing. Some of this modelled writing will demonstrate how to put these ideas into practice; other examples will demonstrate how *not* to do it! There is no better way for your pupils to understand the impact that their writing has on their reader than by exploring the impact that other people's writing has on them.

We are concluding this chapter with a list of 16 generic questions that your pupils can answer about any text you choose to give them. This is a great way to start a lesson or to extend those who finish a task first. Each question relates to one of the chapters of this book and some of them might not be relevant for every text. For example, question 8 is about direct and reported speech, so they might not have much to say for this if they're looking at a piece of non-fiction writing. You could also give these questions to your pupils when they are reading each other's work. It might encourage them to come up with some imaginative feedback for their peers, rather than just the usual half-hearted generalities: 'Your handwriting is nice. You spelled some words wrong.'

Your pupils will need help with answering these questions to begin with. You will need to start by looking at them as a class and modelling the sorts of answers that they might give. In time, they should be able to start tackling them independently after they have read something new. Once they have got into the habit of thinking about these questions regularly, they will become more mindful of their responsibilities to their own readers when they themselves are writing.

1. What do you think is the **purpose** of this text? Is the author trying to persuade you of something? Are they trying to inform you about something? To entertain you? To frighten you? To make you laugh? Does it have another purpose? Has it succeeded in its purpose?

2. What is your **favourite sentence** in the piece of writing? Can you find one that you think has been elegantly crafted and *sounds good*? Can you explain why you chose it? Are there any sentences that you think are a bit clumsy? Can you suggest how they might be improved?

3. Do you think that this piece of writing is the **right length**? Are there any unnecessary words or sentences? Can you find any particularly succinct phrases?

4. Are there any **interesting descriptions** in this piece of writing? Has the author succeeded in putting any pictures or sounds into your mind? How have they done this?

5. Has the author used any particularly **precise nouns and verbs**? Can you give any examples?

6. Are all the sentences the same **length** or are some longer than others? Has this had any impact on the way in which the writing *sounds*?

7. Has the author used any interesting or **unusual sentence structures**? Are there any sentences in the text that you think could be arranged differently?

8. Does the text contain any **speech**, either direct or reported? Do you think that they have used too little or too much of either? Why?

9. How would you describe the **register or tone** of the text? Is it formal or informal? Is it funny or serious? Is it inspiring? Explain your answer with examples.

10. Has the author used any **literary devices** that you're familiar with? For example, can you see any similes, metaphors, repetition, alliteration or rhetorical questions? Did you feel that any of the literary devices used were effective and, if so, in what way?

11. How does this piece of writing make you **feel**? Can you explain how the author has made you feel this way?

12. What do you think about the **structure** of this piece of writing? Did it feel like it was carefully planned and organised? Why/why not?

13. What did you think of **the opening**? Did it make you want to read on? Do you feel that it was a suitable opening now that you've read the rest of the text?

14. Did you feel like the **sentences and paragraphs flowed** together well? If so, can you give an example of the words and phrases that were used to achieve this? If not, can you give an example of something that could have been improved?

15. What were the **themes** of this piece of writing? What was it about? Did it stick to those themes?

16. Did **the ending** come as a surprise? If so, why? Do you think that it was a fitting ending or conclusion to the rest of the text? Why/why not? What did you think of the very last line?

Modelled writing

Mr Nimby

In this chapter, we discussed the importance of distinguishing between sneaky, dishonest persuasive writing (the sort against which we want our pupils to defend themselves) and honest, empathetic persuasive writing (the sort that we want our pupils to produce themselves). An interesting exercise can be generated by this letter, written by a (fictional) grumpy old man during the Second World War, upon hearing that he would be expected to provide a home for evacuees from London. You can discuss the methods of persuasion that he employs with your pupils, but a great task for them is to write a reply to Mr Nimby as a billeting officer, attempting to be sensitive, understanding and polite but also firm when it comes to the issue at hand. This is a great exercise in genuine persuasive writing.

---

1 Stubb Bourne Road
Little Bigoton
Bumbleshire

6 February 1940

Dear Sir/Madam,

   I am writing to express my concern in the strongest possible terms about something I heard on the wireless the other day. According to the six o'clock news bulletin, the authorities are proposing to force residents of Little Bigoton to house evacuees from London in our own homes for an indefinite period of time. While of course we all appreciate the importance of supporting the war effort, this really does strike me as an unnecessarily drastic measure. I wish to outline the basis of my objections in the hope that you might reconsider this decision.

Firstly, it is well known that children from London are loud, malodorous and appallingly behaved. It is not necessarily their fault, of course; city folk have no manners and no sense of decorum, so these deficiencies are inevitably passed on to their offspring. Nonetheless, it is utterly unreasonable to expect decent country folk such as ourselves to accommodate these wild creatures under our own roofs. My elderly mother suffers from a nervous disposition at the best of times and I can only imagine the distress it would cause her to find the sanctuary of her home disturbed by unwashed urban urchins.

No child should be left in danger, however objectionable their conduct or personal hygiene may be. Surely, however, alternative arrangements could be made to house these unfortunate little rogues? All sporting competition has been suspended for the duration of the war; why not house them all in Little Bigoton Cricket Club? There is a kitchen there, as well as bathing facilities. No doubt a few willing local volunteers could be found to look after the children. My mother would be more than happy to donate a few slices of her renowned fruit cake to help feed these unfortunate little creatures.

To conclude, I fully support the war effort and I commend the fine work you are doing to ensure that the country is well prepared for the challenges we face as a nation. This policy, however, is a step too far and I do not believe that you have properly considered the impact it will have on local people. I urge you to reconsider this decision as a matter of urgency.

Yours faithfully,
Mr Peter Nimby

Chapter 2
Macro, micro and middle: The art of the sentence

If you're too young to remember the original National Literacy Strategy, you should probably count yourself lucky on a number of levels. For all its faults, however, one of the strengths of the NLS was that it actively encouraged teachers to give equal weight to word-level, sentence-level and text-level teaching points. A lot of time and energy are exhausted by English teachers on the very big questions about writing (What is it going to be about? How many paragraphs will you need?) or the very small questions (Is it *while* or *whilst*? Do you need a comma here?), but we are often tempted to spend far less time on the questions that lie in the middle (Can I reword this sentence to give it more impact? Have I communicated this point in a way that will be clear to my reader?). These are the questions about how you make your writing *sound good*, and most of this book will focus on them. In order to do that, we must think about that simple and yet most mysterious of concepts: the sentence.

Why it matters

Primary English teachers spend a lot of time and energy on the subject of sentences. First, we encourage children to start each sentence with a capital letter and conclude it with a full stop. As they get older, we might teach them to bring in different types of clause or phrase to make their sentences more complex and sophisticated. There is, however, one thing that we often fail to do quite so well and it's something that seems quite important. We rarely teach children what a sentence actually *is*.

Dictionaries and grammar primers will give you a variety of definitions for the word 'sentence', some of which are too simplistic and some of which are too complicated to be useful. For our purposes, a suitable compromise might be something like:

A sentence is a set of words that is complete in itself. That is to say, it doesn't rely on any other words in order to make sense and none of the other words around it rely on it in order to make sense.

To unpack this a little, consider these three versions of the same sentence(s):

I like. cheese but not ham
I like cheese. but not ham
I like cheese but not ham.

It is apparent to any reader of standard English that only the final iteration of the sentence is punctuated appropriately. If you wanted to explain to a child why the first two full stops are inappropriately positioned, you might be tempted to say something like: 'The full stop goes at the end of the sentence.' However, this is unlikely to be especially helpful feedback. If the child fully understood what you meant by 'the end of the sentence', they probably wouldn't be making these sorts of mistakes in the first place.

However, by reminding them that a sentence doesn't need any other words in order to make sense, and that none of the other words need *it* in order to make sense, you can start to explain exactly what you mean. In the first example, the words 'I like' have no meaning on their own. They are only given meaning by the presence of the four words that follow the full stop. Therefore, they are not a complete sentence. In the second example, 'I like cheese' could be an entirely valid sentence on its own (which shows you exactly why children can find it hard to understand where one sentence ends and another begins) but there's still a problem. While 'I like cheese' is all right, Jack, its buddies can't get to the party. By ending the sentence immediately after the first three words, we are leaving the words 'but not ham' isolated and without meaning. Here, some adults might be tempted to tell a child that the reason you can't put a full stop here is because it's 'wrong to start a sentence with "but"'. But, unfortunately, this is not true; starting a sentence (like the one you're reading right now) with the word 'but' can be a perfectly legitimate stylistic choice.

Sentences typically include at least one subject and at least one verb. Usually, that verb forms part of an extended phrase, known as a predicate, indicating what the subject is, does or experiences. Let's look at another straightforward example:

Ruth ran all the way home.

What is the subject of this sentence? It's *Ruth*. Why? Because it was Ruth who ran all the way home. What is the predicate in this sentence? It's 'ran all the way home'. Why? Because it describes what Ruth was, did or experienced in this sentence and it contains the main verb – *ran*. Many sentences contain more than one clause and may contain multiple subjects, each with their own predicate. If you're not clear on the role of the subject and verb in English, Chapters 4 and 5 of *The Grammar Book* will be a helpful place to start.

A sentence (like the one above) that contains just one clause is known as a simple sentence. A sentence that contains multiple clauses, each with their own subject and main verb, is known as a complex sentence. It's interesting that we always seem to teach children about sentences before we teach them about clauses when, in many ways, a clause is a simpler concept. We're probably just impatient to make sure that the capital letters and the full stops go in the right places!

So, we've established what sentences *are*. Now we come to an equally fundamental question: what are sentences *for*? A sentence, very simply, communicates an idea. An idea can refer to anything, from the utterly banal to our deepest philosophical musings:

This chair is slightly uncomfortable.
I love you.
We are mortal and nothing lasts forever, but I believe that the impermanent fragility of life is precisely what makes it valuable.

Each of these three sentences conveys an idea and each one does so in a way that is designed to make it easy to read and straightforward to understand. As you can probably imagine, the first two sentences required less conscious thought to construct than the third. However, all three are 'good sentences' – they communicate one idea clearly, vividly and without excessive ambiguity. Crucially, they are also all fairly easy to read for someone with a decent knowledge of English vocabulary.

Many people assume that a good sentence is simply a combination of good grammar, accurate spelling and some fancy words. This is why many teachers will sometimes look at a child's writing and find it difficult to identify how it can be improved, even though they can clearly see that the child in question isn't Ian McEwan yet. Sometimes it can be because the sentence feels clumsy or because it requires effort to read. You know that feeling when you pick up a child's book in order to read a long piece of writing that they've produced and your heart sinks because you know it's going to be *hard to read*? Sure you do. Typically, teachers will give feedback like 'make sure you read back over your work and check it makes sense'. The problem is that lots of it probably *does* make sense – it's just clumsy. Children's academic and social development aren't always as inseparable as we like to imagine. Part of being a good writer is being able to exhibit empathy towards your reader – to imagine what it would be like to read the words that you yourself have written. That can be very difficult for many children. What we often mean when we say that a sentence is poorly written is that the writer hasn't taken the time to make it accessible – in short, the reader is being made to do all the work.

How to do it

How do we make a sentence easy to read? You might think that it's all about the length and complexity of the sentence or the level of vocabulary employed. These factors can certainly play a part but there are other little tricks that you can use to make your sentences easily accessible to your reader. The good news is that most of these can be made accessible to your pupils too.

Firstly, it is important to acknowledge that, of course, much of this is subjective. Just as different people find satisfaction in different forms of art or music, so they will differ in their tastes when it comes to the arrangement of words in a sentence. However, just because our viewpoints are subjective, that doesn't mean that they're arbitrary. Even if classical music isn't really your thing, you would no doubt acknowledge the genius of Mozart and Beethoven and you would recognise that the music they composed is, on some agreed level, *good*. Equally, we all had friends when we were teenagers who formed bands and made music that no one, even their own parents, would have been willing to describe in terms any more favourable than 'interesting' or 'different'. The same is true of writing. Reading an entire classic novel might not be everyone's idea of fun nowadays but it would be utterly petulant to claim that Jane Austen or Charles Dickens were not exceptionally talented writers. Equally, we all know people whose written communication is objectively clumsy and requires effort on the part of the reader.

When talented composers create music, they do so in full awareness of the musical culture that we all share. They know that major keys will sound more triumphant and that minor keys will sound sad. They know that they will create a certain feeling of satisfaction if the piece of music ends on the tonic (i.e. the root note) of the key it started in. There is, however, no set of conventions a composer can follow that is guaranteed to produce music that a listener will enjoy. There are also countless musicians who made their names precisely by defying convention entirely. The point is that the conventions exist and even the great jazz musicians understood the rules that they were breaking. Writing is no different. When we adhere to certain conventions, we make our words accessible to the reader. Competent adult writers follow these conventions without thinking. Children, on the other hand, may need to have them pointed out.

Examples of writing conventions

Now we're going to look at some simple principles that will usually help us to write good sentences. None of these are conventions that we should adhere to *all* the time, but they will make us better writers if we adhere to them *most* of the time.

Let's start with something very common but not always easy to spot. We could easily imagine a child in Year 6 writing something like this:

> **A girl who was in my class when I was in Year 2 but who left at the start of Year 3 and whose name I've forgotten is going to my new secondary school.**

Generally speaking, we'd probably be pretty happy if all our Year 6 pupils could write like this. The spelling, grammar and punctuation are all fine. But aren't we aware, nonetheless, that something here still feels a little bit clumsy? If you look for the subject and the main verb, you might realise why this sentence is difficult to read. The subject, *a girl*, is introduced at the start of the sentence and corresponds to the main verb phrase *is going*. There are 25 words in between the two and that is just too many. When we read sentences, we expect the main verb to follow fairly briskly on from the subject of the sentence. Sometimes, there will be stylistic reasons why we don't adhere to this convention but, in the example above, it just looks as though the sentence has been crafted a bit lazily. A sentence like this would be better divided up into several clauses, so that each subject can be placed close to the corresponding main verb:

> **I'm going to the same secondary school as a girl who was in my class when I was in Year 2, although she left at the start of Year 3 and I've forgotten her name.**

Anyone who is used to reading English will agree that the new version of the sentence is clearer and easier to read. The subject and the main verb of the first clause have been moved about as close together as possible – *I* and *am* have been contracted into a single word. The sentence now contains three additional clauses and, in every case, the subject and the main verb are reassuringly close together. All of this is fairly simple to explain to children whose knowledge of grammar is good. If they know what clauses are, if they understand what we mean by the subject of the sentence and if they can identify verbs, then you can easily explain to them how to improve their sentences using that terminology. This is why we think it's important for children to learn about grammar – not simply for its own sake but because, in the right hands, English grammar terminology helps teachers to make their pupils into better writers. But we digress!

As well as placing the subject and the main verb close together, we usually position both of them close to the beginning of the sentence or clause. If you don't believe us, look at this example:

In three rows of eight, with spaces of about 5 cm between each one, and far enough away from the house that they got plenty of sunlight, the daffodils were growing.

In the example above, both the subject (*daffodils*) and the main verb phrase (*were growing*) appear right at the end of the sentence. As a consequence, reading the sentence feels like something of an effort. You are forced to remember a lot of information before you find out what that information is about. Look at what happens if you arrange the sentence in a more orthodox way:

The daffodils were growing in three rows of eight, with spaces of about 5 cm between each one, and far enough away from the house that they got plenty of sunlight.

Placing the subject and main verb at the beginning actually makes the sentence *easier to read*. The reader immediately knows that the sentence is about daffodils growing, and the rest of the information merely adds to that picture.

Reading is hard cognitive work and it's easier when we only have to move in one direction. When the wording of a sentence is clumsy or ambiguous, we might have to reread it several times. Good sentences keep us moving through the text in one forward direction – they *flow*. Of course, even when we're reading the most beautifully written text in the world, we might sometimes lose concentration and have to go back over it again. In general, however, a good sentence makes its meaning apparent on the first attempt.

Look at this sentence:

After changes to the curriculum, children studied in history lessons included Anne Frank.

This is known as a 'garden path sentence'. You were probably slightly thrown by it for a moment. Readers of English have certain expectations of the sentences that they read. For example, we usually expect the subject of each clause to appear straight away and to be fairly brief. We then expect the main verb to follow soon afterwards. The sentence above consists of a fronted adverbial (*after changes to the curriculum*) and then a main clause (*children studied in history lessons included Anne Frank*). When reading the sentence for the first time, your brain will have registered the fronted adverbial and felt reassured that you were reading a standard English sentence, employing simple and predictable grammatical structures. In less than a second, you will have moved onto the main clause and felt reassured to see that it began with a noun and a verb (*children studied*). You will have assumed, incorrectly, that you were looking at a subject and its predicate. Instead, the clause contains a long-winded subject (*children studied in history lessons*) and the main verb is *included*. Your first instinct will have been to assume that *children* referred to children doing the studying, not children being studied. You had been led up the garden path, so to speak. Good writers avoid doing this sort of thing to their readers, unless there is a deliberate stylistic reason to try to pull them up short.

Here is another well-known example of a garden path sentence that you may have encountered before:

The complex houses married and single soldiers and their families.

If you haven't encountered this example before, and you're still struggling to make sense of it, try this rewording:

The complex provides housing for soldiers, both married and single, along with their families.

Why do we find the original sentence so confusing when we read it for the first time? A lot of it comes down to the fact that so many English words can belong to different word classes in different contexts. So, for example, the word *complex* is being used as a noun in the sentence above, but you may have read it as an adjective. The word *houses* is being used as a verb, but you may have read it as a noun. The word *married* is being used as an adjective, but you may have read it as a verb.

The other problem with the sentence above is its overreliance on the conjunction *and*. You have a situation where the word *and* is being used to separate two adjectives in the phrase *married and single soldiers* but then it is used again to separate that entire phrase from the final phrase: *their families*. It's usually a good idea to avoid using *and* more than once in each clause. Alternatives such as *along with* or *as well as* give you some other options when linking two phrases, one of which already contains the word *and* (as in the example above).

All of these tricks serve to eliminate ambiguity – that is to say, to ensure that your sentence has only one plausible meaning. This is harder than it sounds. Many words and phrases have more than one possible interpretation and we all know how easy it is to misread the intended intonation in other people's written messages. It's often said that we Brits are particularly prone to this sort of thing as we so rarely say what we mean. In our everyday vernacular, the phrase 'can't complain' can mean anything, from 'I've just won the lottery' to 'I'm literally on fire right now'. This is why the art of crafting a good sentence is such an important part of writing.

Feedback

How, then, does all this help you to give feedback to your pupils? Hopefully, it does so in a number of ways. Firstly, most teachers are very competent writers but they're often not consciously aware of the conventions to which they adhere when they put pen to paper. The contents of this chapter might help to unravel some of the mystery about how we form straightforward sentences.

The next time that you're reading a pupil's work and the sentences just seem a little bit clumsy, and you can't put your finger on the reason for it, try working through this checklist:

- **Does the sentence contain an identifiable subject?**
- **Is the subject close to the beginning of the sentence?**
- **Does the sentence contain an identifiable main verb or main verb phrase?**
- **Is the main verb close to the beginning of the sentence?**
- **Are the subject and the main verb close together?**
- **Does the sentence flow, i.e. did I have to go back and reread it? If so, why?**
- **Did the sentence lead me up the 'garden path' and, if so, why?**
- **Did the sentence contain ambiguity? If so, why?**

If you can empower your pupils to work through this checklist themselves, then the impact will be even greater. Obviously, this means making sure that their understanding of grammar is pretty solid. If you need to go back and make sure that they're clear on what we mean by the subject of the sentence or the definitions of different word classes, then do it. Sometimes you have to go backwards to move forwards.

Editing

Children can only really master the art of the sentence if they get into the habit of editing their own writing. Part of the problem with this, as every English teacher knows, is that some children just don't really know what editing is. Some pupils might pass an entirely uncritical eye over the words that they've already written, get to the end and say that they've finished. Others might at least do you the honour of proofreading their own work and spotting a couple of spelling errors or omitted words. It's actually very hard to get children to look back at their own writing and stand in the shoes of an impartial reader. However, there are a few ways in which we can help to get them doing it.

First, try asking them to edit some work that they did quite a long time ago – not the previous day or even the previous week, but perhaps something that they wrote six months ago. It's a very different experience. Have you ever found poetry, diary entries, letters or song lyrics that you wrote when you were a teenager? If the answer is 'yes', you probably winced just thinking about it. We're much more critical of ourselves when a significant amount of time has passed, and six months is an eternity when you're 11. In fact, if you present most children with something that they wrote quite a long time ago, they'll be *keen* to edit it because they'll want to prove how far they've come in the time that has elapsed! If you gradually start to reduce the time between writing and editing, you can eventually teach your pupils to pass a critical eye over something that they finished writing 30 seconds ago.

As with anything that we do in the classroom, you need to provide appropriate prompts and scaffolds. You might want to give your pupils specific things to look for. The checklist above is useful with a class who have got used to doing this, but you'll want to start with something simpler. You could ask your pupils to go through and identify the subject and the main verb in each of their sentences. Ask whether anyone would be willing to volunteer an example of a sentence where the subject and main verb are particularly far apart. If you think that it's appropriate and the child happily consents to their writing being used in this way, you could use it as a prompt for discussion and see whether anyone else in the class can suggest a way to help them to edit that particular sentence.

At the time of writing, there is a peculiar disconnect between the way in which children write at school and the way in which almost all adults write in the real world. The vast majority of writing in our society is produced on a keyboard using software that enables us to constantly draft and revise our sentences with the greatest of ease. The majority of children's writing in school is done with a pen or a pencil. It's hard to believe that this is entirely sustainable and it's hard to know exactly when and how this is going to change. It's clearly important that children still have the opportunity to learn to write by hand, but it's also true that if you want children to be able to habitually edit and refine their sentences, a word processor is going to have to be part of the story. Think about the last lengthy piece of writing you did that you wanted to get just right. Maybe it was an email to a colleague, a personal statement for a job application or even a speech for a wedding. The likelihood is that you typed it. Now imagine that you had handwritten it and that every little alteration, correction and amendment had been rubbed out or crossed out. The page would have been a mess, and yet children are generally praised when their English books are reasonably tidy. That's a tricky circle to square but, for the moment, it's probably sufficient to say that we should give children plenty of opportunities to type their work. It will help them to craft their sentences with care and precision.

Summary

As teachers, we spend a lot of time reminding children to write in full sentences. However, we sometimes neglect to actually teach them what sentences are. There are several tricks that our pupils can use to form elegant, well-crafted sentences, but they will first need to master the basics of sentence-level grammar: subject, verb and object. Rather than seeing a good sentence as something that includes a checklist of features, you want your pupils to think about readability. A good sentence is easy to read and easy to understand.

Where next?

In this chapter we've established an agreed definition of a sentence and explored some of the common errors that your pupils might make when constructing their sentences. The resources and modelled writing at the end of this chapter can be used to support your pupils with sentence construction. The next chapter covers how you can teach your pupils to have the maximum impact in as few words as possible. It's about being succinct.

Resources and modelled texts

These resources are for those pupils who need an extra challenge – when you really want to make them think about sentence construction. Here is a paragraph about fishing. The sentences are clumsy and beset by the many sins described in this chapter. Try giving this paragraph to a group of pupils and see whether they can tell what needs changing:

> **My grandad and me and also sometimes his friend who he's been friends with for over 50 years fish in a river near my house. Although you may not think they're very interesting or maybe you think you already know a lot about them, and for all I know maybe you're right, I like learning about all the fish. Fish in the river like me and you learn about food chains. You may not realise there are fish fish eat and there are even fish fish fish eat eat. However, because they're bigger we prefer to fish fish don't eat. Sometimes we'll fish fish fish eat but, because they're so small, we never fish fish fish fish eat eat.**

Children can have a lot of fun with this, especially once they realise that it does make perfect grammatical sense! If you need it, here is a clearer translation:

> **I go fishing near my house with my grandad, and he sometimes brings his friend of over 50 years. Fish are more interesting than you might realise and I like learning about them. Because I go fishing, I learn a lot about food chains. You may not know that some fish eat other smaller fish, and sometimes those smaller fish eat even tinier ones. We prefer to catch the biggest fish at the top of the food chain. We're sometimes pleased to catch the fish in the middle of the food chain too, but we don't tend to go for the tiny ones.**

The ending is essentially our own version of Dmitri Borgmann's famous garden path sentence:

> **Buffalo buffalo Buffalo buffalo buffalo buffalo Buffalo buffalo.**

To unpick that one, you have to understand that, as a noun, a buffalo is both an animal and (with a capital B) a city in America. As a verb, it can mean to bully someone or to confuse someone. You can therefore interpret the sentence like this:

> **A herd of buffalo from the city of Buffalo are being bullied by other buffalo from the same city. The victims of this bullying are a source of confusion to their tormentors.**

If this doesn't prove to your pupils that sentence construction matters, then nothing will!

Chapter 3
Less is more: Being succinct

Instinctively, many children will write as they speak during everyday conversations. At first glance, this may seem both obvious and unproblematic. However, it really is important that they understand the differences between the conventions of speech and the conventions of writing. Speaking and writing are not the same – not even nearly. Whenever you encounter a written transcript of a real conversation in a news story (an account of a witness being cross-examined in a court case, for example), you'll find that it's surprisingly hard to follow. Much of the meaning is communicated through body language or intonation and much of the heavy lifting is performed by phrases that hardly appear at all in written English. Just think about the number of different meanings you can convey by varying the manner and timing of utterances like 'right', 'you know' or 'well'. We don't usually speak in full sentences – most of the things that we say when talking informally with one another are fragments of sentences, brief phrases or single words. Even if it were possible to do this when we write, it would cause confusion and make the act of reading harder. Writing has to grab the reader and immediately bring them face to face with the point that you are trying to make or the idea that you wish to explore. This is a subtle difference to explain to children. How are we to communicate it? The answer lies in teaching them to be succinct.

Why it matters

When we're having a spoken conversation with someone, we're not only exchanging information and perspectives. We're also, more often than not, seeking to build and deepen our bond with another person – not just to understand their point of view or the information that they are trying to convey, but to understand *them*. Even in relatively formal settings such as a staff meeting or a job interview, spoken conversations are full of cues and nuances that are all about the participants' relationships with, and feelings about, one another. This often means that we actually take longer to say things than we need to, especially in sensitive situations, such as that moment when a colleague comes up with a truly terrible idea and you feel that you need to gently offer a counterpoint! Even when having a relaxed chat with your oldest friend, you'll probably pepper your conversations with unnecessary words and phrases that reinforce the connection between you and make everyone feel at ease. When TV scriptwriters want to depict emotionless characters, such as the Vulcans in *Star Trek* and Sheldon from *The Big Bang Theory*, they will often make the dialogue for those characters uncomfortably or even comically precise and direct. This is because spoken English is not usually precise and direct. Good writing, however, is.

As children begin a piece of written work, they will often ask their teacher *how long* it should be. It can be tempting to give a finite, measurable answer such as 'about a page'. Alternatively, you might offer an answer such as 'about three hundred words' if you want to avoid conferring unfair advantage based on the size of a child's handwriting or their choice of font size! There is, however, a problem with both approaches. Inevitably, even when the children doing a task at school are conscientious and motivated, their primary aim is often to *get it done*. Why wouldn't it be? We all approach many of the jobs that we have to do in this way, whether we're adults or children. Only very occasionally do we apply utterly meticulous precision to a task. If a child knows that a piece of writing needs to be a certain length, they will have no incentive to make their sentences lean and efficient. Instead, they are likely to produce clumsy, repetitive, downright boring writing simply to finish the page or hit the word limit. Sometimes, this can be hard to spot and it can be even harder to 'correct'. For example, imagine encountering this opening to a story in a child's work:

> **There were once two sisters named Emily and Sarah. Emily was older than Sarah. Sarah was a bit irresponsible and she was always running off or getting lost. One day, Emily and Sarah decided to go to the funfair. When they arrived, they saw that it was full of people. After a while, Emily realised that Sarah was missing. She looked all around her but she couldn't see her anywhere.**

What feedback would you offer a child who produced an opening like this? They've introduced their characters and their setting, and they've created a problem that will need to be solved later in the story. Their grammar and spelling are flawless. In fact, it may seem pretty hard to find any fault with this at all. If that is your instinct, try something else. Try imagining that you picked up a published work of children's fiction and found the same opening. What would be your instincts now? Doesn't it seem a little bit flat, clumsy and amateurish? If so, the reason is probably that it is far longer than it needs to be. All of the information in that paragraph could, in fact, be communicated in a single sentence:

> **Emily scanned the busy crowds at the funfair but, as usual, her little sister Sarah was nowhere to be seen.**

The first, longer version tugs half-heartedly at the reader's sleeve. The second version grabs the reader by the scruff of the neck and hauls them straight into the action. The reason for this is simple: every word and phrase in that one sentence is working hard. The sentence itself conveys an entire scenario, not merely a single fact. Put simply, the second version is more succinct.

Now, you may be thinking that this is a pretty strange priority, especially so early in our book. Your job, after all, is to create decent Key Stage 2 or 3 writers, not fully formed authors of marketable children's fiction. Good things happen, however, when we look at children's writing through the prism of succinctness right from the outset, as we will see repeatedly throughout this book. In the first chapter, we looked at making sentences easy to read. In this chapter, we're looking at how to communicate as much as possible without writing more than we need to. Writing that does both these things, with accurate spelling, appropriate grammar and an entertaining theme, will be 'good writing'. That's not just our opinion – it would be almost anyone's opinion, even if they don't fully understand why. Being succinct isn't a luxurious afterthought upon which we should leave children to ponder later on. On the contrary, it is a fundamental principle that should guide every choice that we (and our pupils) make when writing.

If you're still not convinced, let's come at this issue from the opposite direction. Read this sentence:

> **Unperturbed by either of his previous defeats, the King returned the following spring and successfully besieged the enemy capital.**

Presumably, we can all agree that we'd be pretty chuffed if a child in our class offered up a sentence like that. Ask yourself why. Is it the vocabulary? Partly, perhaps, but only *unperturbed* and *besieged* are unusually advanced words for Key Stage 2. Is it the grammar? Perhaps you could argue that it contains a pleasingly original fronted adverbial phrase, but there is nothing hugely unusual about the structure of the sentence. What really punches the reader in the nose is the sheer amount of information conveyed by the writer's language choices: an epic saga in 19 words.

Notice too that nobody would actually speak like this in everyday conversation. Perhaps the presenter of a television documentary or an academic delivering a carefully prepared lecture might utter a sentence of this sort, but it would clearly indicate that the speaker was reading or reciting something that had, at some point, been *written*. Succinctness is the hallmark of competent writing, and yet all too often we actively discourage it with the messages that we give to children.

How to do it

Lean sentences

So, how do we help children to make their writing more succinct? Well, first it might be a good idea to explore what *not* to do. For a start, don't encourage your pupils to pepper their writing with clutter, e.g. pointless adjectives and adverbs (see the next chapter) that serve only to make their writing clumsier. Secondly, try to resist the temptation to set finite targets in terms of 'how much' writing children need to produce. This is something that they'll need to do when they're writing essays at university, but if you teach them to write with control now, they'll find it much easier when the time comes. Finally, encourage them to reflect on the structure of every sentence that they write. To do this, they need to have a solid understanding of the subject–verb–object (or subject and predicate) relationship. If you don't feel that you have a solid understanding of this yourself, it would be a good idea to go back and look at Chapter 1. You can read more about subjects, verbs and objects in Chapter 5 of *The Grammar Book*.

The most succinct sentences that we can possibly write are those that consist of a subject, a main verb and nothing else:

> **Smoking kills.**
> **The truth hurts.**
> **Hot air rises.**
> **Money talks.**
> **S**t happens.**

In each of these cases, both the subject (in the form of a noun) and the verb have been carefully chosen to convey as much meaning as possible. As a result, each of these five sentences carries a very strong but very efficient message. Of course, you don't want your pupils to write predominantly in two- or three-word sentences, but you should encourage them to start with their subject and main verb, adding to it only what they actually need their reader to know.

Combining sentences

Most sentences, of course, do require more than just a subject and a verb. Chapters 9 to 15 of *The Grammar Book* deal with the various ways in which you can do this, but our concern now is not with *how* to extend sentences but *when* and *why* they might need extending.

Very often, a sentence can be extended to consume the sentence(s) before or after it. Here is a very simple example:

> **Arnav likes butter.**
> **Arnav is my brother.**   →   **Arnav, my older brother, likes butter.**
> **Arnav is older than me.**

When giving feedback on a pupil's writing, try highlighting a few dull, cumbersome sentences and challenging pupils to rewrite that section as a single sentence. Very often, a teacher's instinct can be to do the opposite – to take one perfectly acceptable sentence that they've written and make it even longer.

Time limits only

Next time your pupils ask you how long their writing should be, insist on giving only a timeframe, e.g. 'it should be 30 minutes long'. At first, they'll do that annoying thing where they curl their upper lip, jerk their head backwards and look at you like you're an idiot. However, if you are insistent and persistent, they will get used to the idea that any piece of writing should be the best that they can do in X minutes. Now, we know what you're thinking because we'd be thinking it too. You're picturing that child who will use this stipulation as an excuse to write only three lines. With them, there are two possibilities. One (the most likely one) is that their writing is going to be seriously lacking something. If it's a story, they probably haven't engaged their reader and made them connect with a character or picture the setting. If it's a piece of non-fiction writing, then it is probably not very informative or persuasive. That, therefore, should be your feedback.

However, what do you do with a child who produces three lines that address the task perfectly when others have written an entire page? Our advice would be to say a warm 'well done' and encourage the other pupils in the class to look closely at how they achieved it.

In the next section, you'll find modelled writing and resources that you can use with your class to help them to make their writing more succinct.

Summary

Succinctness matters. Make it happen!

Where next?

As always, there are supporting resources at the end of this chapter. This is the final chapter of Part One. So far, we have covered why we write and how writing has evolved, and explored the concept of the sentence in greater detail. The next section is all about the words that you choose to put in your sentences, and how you choose to structure your writing. Onward.

Resources and modelled texts

Single-sentence fairytales

Challenge your class to retell a classic fairytale using just a single sentence. The sentence can contain multiple clauses but it must be grammatically correct (not run-on sentences!). A task like this takes the focus off thinking of what to write and puts it on *how* to write it instead. Start by giving your class a few examples:

> **After pricking her finger on a spinning wheel, a girl falls asleep for a hundred years and is eventually woken by a kiss from a prince.**

> **Despite her stepmother's best attempts to stop her, a young girl attends a ball, where she falls in love with a prince.**

After they have come up with a few of their own, use your pupils' examples as a springboard for a discussion about being succinct. Discussion questions you could use:

- Which parts of the story did you decide to include? What did you leave out?
- Why did you choose this word? What does it convey? What other words could you have used there?
- Is there any way that you could make this sentence shorter and keep the meaning the same?
- If I said that you were allowed to use a second sentence, what other information would you have included?

Poetry

Exploring different poetry structures with your class will challenge them to be concise. For example, can they write a haiku – with a structure of five syllables on the first line, seven on the second and five on the third? For example:

> When you are writing
> It is important to be
> Succinct and precise

Or challenge them to write a Shakespearean sonnet with ten syllables written in iambic pentameter in each line, or a cinquain poem with five lines and the following structure:

Line 1: two syllables

Line 2: four syllables

Line 3: six syllables

Line 4: eight syllables

Line 5: two syllables

While they may find such restrictive structures frustrating, it will focus your pupils on which words really matter.

Modelled writing

There are a number of things that you could do with the following short story. You could simply read it and, as a class, discuss how it could be more succinct. You could get your pupils to rewrite the story, ensuring that they keep the meaning the same but cutting out the unnecessary information. You could challenge them to tell the exact same story in as few words as possible. (The story at the moment is 629 words.)

The arrival

Around the farm, all the animals were discussing it. The ducks had overheard the farmer talking about it on the phone; they had told the pigs, who had told the cows and the cows had told the horses. The horses, who considered themselves rather aloof and above all such nonsense, had refused to engage and had not passed it on but, as is always the way, the news spread. A new animal was going to arrive at the farm next week. No one knew exactly what sort of animal it was going to be but around the farmyard rumours were spreading.

'Well, I heard the farmer say it could arrive any day now,' clucked the chickens.

'Yes, I heard it was next week,' replied the ducks. 'Around 6 lb he said on the phone – that's too heavy for a duck – I think it must be a goose.'

'Or a piglet?' the sow piped up from her pen.

It's not that the animals were worried about this new arrival; it's just that so little happened on the farm day to day that this news was incredibly exciting, and speculating about what sort of animal it might be became a full-time hobby. It had been a long time since there had been any new additions to the farm, other than the lambs that had arrived last spring.

'Well, where is this new animal going to sleep? I'm not sharing the barn,' the horses announced, gruffly. The horses weren't very good at sharing.

'I hope they're not going to be taking our share of the food,' the pigs wondered aloud.

This chatter continued all week, although the farmer was mostly oblivious. He seemed rather preoccupied. He would still remember to feed the animals each morning and evening, he still collected the eggs and baled the hay, but his mind seemed elsewhere. Often, he would chat away happily to his animals as he worked, telling them about the jobs he was doing on the farm, asking them their opinion, etc. They never replied, of course, but it didn't stop him. This week, the farmer was suspiciously quiet and his behaviour was increasingly erratic. He was awake at strange times, and one evening he even set off in his car at 9.00 pm and still hadn't returned by 4.00 am. This was very out of character and it worried the animals.

'What if the reason he is acting so strangely is he is planning to replace us with this new arrival?' the cow asked in a panic one evening.

'Don't be ridiculous – how could he possibly replace all of us?' replied the donkey.

'Well – I don't know what is going on but I just hope he isn't getting a cat,' the barn mouse squeaked. (Barn mice are not particularly fond of cats.)

'Quiet everyone – listen!' barked the dog.

The animals strained to hear the sound of a car pulling up on the gravel driveway.

'He's back! Oh, thank goodness.' The goose breathed a sigh of relief.

The farmer stepped out of the car, quietly closing the door behind him. He then walked around to the other side of the car and opened the door to let out his wife. Then they both went to the back door of the car, opened it, leaned inside and started speaking in hushed tones to a carrier on the back seat.

'They're back and with the new animal!' alerted the cockerel.

The animals gathered around the fence and peered over, trying to get a glimpse at the new arrival.

The farmer stepped back to allow his wife to pass with the carrier. He looked up at the animals, his eyes full of pride.

'Everyone – meet the new member of the family. This is my baby daughter, Jess.'

Part Two

Selecting words and arranging your writing

Chapter 4

Powerfully powerless: Describing things

Think about your English curriculum. How much of it is dedicated to teaching descriptive techniques? In every school in which we have worked, a significant amount of lesson time has been dedicated to similes, metaphors, alliteration, personification and powerful adjectives, while tasks such as setting and character descriptions seem to dominate schemes of work.

It's not that descriptive writing doesn't matter; it's more that the amount of time it is given in our curriculum is disproportionate, given that most of the writing they will do when they're older will be essays, reports and other forms of persuasive writing, such as job and university applications. That's not to say that we shouldn't teach descriptive writing as a creative pursuit and just for the love of it. However, if we are going to dedicate so much time to teaching descriptive writing, let's at least teach it right.

Why it matters

In the last chapter, we looked at the value of eliminating pointless clutter from children's writing. A great place to start in this endeavour is with adjectives and adverbs. Whatever you may see on teachers' planning up and down the country, there is no such thing as a powerful adjective (or adverb). Adjectives modify nouns and pronouns (adverbs modify verbs or adjectives) and they make them as powerful, as weak, as big, as small, as luminescent or as, say, antidisestablishmentarian as you want them to be.

For some reason, adjectives have gained a special status in some primary schools as a silver bullet that will instantly improve the quality of your writing. And we're not talking about adjectives such as tall, short, big and small, no – children are encouraged to think of the longest, most elaborate adjective that they can. Why have a *small green door* when you can have a *minuscule eau de Nil entrance*?

The truth is, too many adjectives will make your pupils' writing clunky and difficult to read, particularly if your priority is using flowery vocabulary. Or, to put it another way:

When the lexicon deployed by the progenitor of a literary creation is excessively pretentious, the consumer of the product will invariably discover that comprehension and apprehension of the author's intention is hindered by the unimaginable exhaustion inherent in undertaking to instantiate such a bewildering array of linguistic flourishes.

But don't just take our word for it. One of our favourite anecdotes is the story of a Roald Dahl fan who sent him some of her short stories. His response?

> *'Eschew all these beastly adjectives! Surely it is better to say, "She was a tall girl with a bosom" than "She was a tall girl with a shapely, prominent bosom," or some such rubbish. The first one says it all.'* (Roald Dahl, 1980, in Wyatt, 2017)

While it was a rather direct response and the example that Dahl uses is not one that you would necessarily use with your primary school pupils, the principle is sound. So how do we teach descriptive writing without creating children who believe that an adjective is the hallmark of good literature?

How to do it

Share these three questions with your pupils and encourage them to reflect on them when they are writing:

1. What am I describing?
2. Why am I describing it?
3. How am I describing it?

Let's explore each one in turn:

What am I describing?

You may remember from our rant about adjectives in *The Grammar Book* that one common problem is pupils using adjectives that tell the reader what they already know, e.g. 'the big grey elephant'. In that case, the feedback to the child was that the word 'elephant' is utterly unchanged by adding 'big' and 'grey' to the front of it and that, unless the elephant was 3 cm high and had polka dot skin, it probably didn't need an adjective at all.

Adjectives, like most descriptive techniques, are a tool, and we should be teaching our pupils to use them discerningly. They do not need an adjective for every noun; they won't even need one in every sentence. We need to teach them to be selective when choosing what to describe.

A quick way in which to demonstrate this to your class is to ask them to pick up their nearest fiction text and turn to any page. You could use the modelled writing on page 45 for this, but we find that this tends to have a greater impact when all the pupils are using a different text. Ask them to count the number of nouns and the number of adjectives on that page. Even in the most description-heavy text, the nouns will far outweigh the adjectives, and this should bring home how selective your pupils need to be with their description in order to write like a writer.

Why am I describing it?

Closely linked to 'what am I describing?' is 'why am I describing it?' Here, the focus for our pupils should be on the purpose of their description: what do they want to add to the reader's perception of the noun or the verb in question? If our pupils are using adjectives in their writing, there should be a reason for it. Just as we know that the elephant is big and grey, we know that the old man probably has wrinkled skin and we know that the sun is hot; don't waste words on telling the reader what they already know. Instead, teach your pupils to focus on what it is they want their reader to understand about the character or setting through their choice of description.

For example, if I tell you that 'Mr Jones sat down in his old, battered leather armchair', what impression does that give you of Mr Jones? The reader might assume that because the chair is old, Mr Jones is older – maybe he's had the armchair for a while and is quite attached to it. The fact that the armchair is described as 'battered' suggests that it is probably time to replace it, but Mr Jones either doesn't want to or can't afford to.

Now consider how your impression of Mr Jones changes if I write that he sat down in his 'sleek black ergonomic office chair'. We immediately imagine the character to be a couple of decades younger and someone who spends a lot of their time working, perhaps with more money to spend on expensive furniture.

Of course, it could be that the chair isn't important to the story and doesn't tell us much about the character at all; in which case, describe something else in the room that tells the reader about the character, plot or setting. The main point is to teach your pupils that if they are describing something in detail, it should be for a reason. Activity A in the resources section allows your pupils to explore how being precise with their adjectives can alter the reader's perception of a character.

How am I describing it?

This question should be the easiest one to answer if your pupils have thought carefully enough about the other two questions.

If your pupil has a clear understanding of what they are describing and why, then this question should answer itself. They'll know the language that they need to use to build up the reader's impression of the setting or character. Once again, it comes back to 'what do you want your reader to know?' Adjectives help to build pictures in the reader's mind; you want those pictures to be clear. So, let's unpack this a bit.

If you write that a bed is 'magnificent and delightful', the reader knows that you like it. But if you say that a bed is 'warm and soft', the reader stills know that you like it, but they also understand why you like it and the whole description feels more real.

Once again, this demonstrates the problem that we've created by focusing on 'wow' words; warm and soft are simple tier-one vocabulary, but the sentence reads much more naturally with these adjectives. A reminder: adjectives themselves are not powerful – they modify nouns. As writers, your pupils have the power to use adjectives to develop the reader's impression of their characters, setting and plot.

Feedback

Breaking description down into the 'what, why and how' will not only help your pupils with their writing but will also provide you with a structure for giving feedback. When you're going through your pupils' work, ask yourself which of these questions they have not thought carefully enough about. Here are some questions that you could use in a feedback discussion with your pupils:

- Was there a reason why this noun needed this description?
- What does this tell the reader that they didn't already know?
- Why did you choose this adjective/adverb? Was it your first choice?
- What would be the impact if you removed this adjective/adverb from your sentence?

Those questions are just the starting point, and you'll find other examples of discussion questions throughout the book. For a few pupils, just having these discussions and asking those questions will be enough to prompt them to review their own work and edit it accordingly. For the vast majority, you will need to model this for them – not just by showing them a perfect modelled example, but by modelling the process of taking a piece of descriptive writing and editing it, cutting out adjectives and discussing with your class why you're removing them. The modelled text 'The jungle' on page 45 would be a useful starting point for this.

Your pupils may find it helpful to have a copy of the following common errors to refer to when they are editing their descriptive writing. Obviously, this is not an exhaustive list, but in our experience the problems with children's descriptive writing tend to fall into the categories discussed in the following section.

Common errors

There are a few common errors that pupils will make when they first start using adjectives. In this section, we'll address each in turn and think about the feedback and, in some cases, the resources that your pupils might need to improve their writing.

1. Adjective pile-up

We're probably all familiar with this one; it's sentences like this:

The big, heavy, green dinosaurs trampled over the hot, dusty, red ground and let out a loud, scary roar.

Every noun has multiple adjectives piled up in front of it. Eventually, you would hope to move your pupil on from adding an adjective to every noun, but for now just focus on getting them to choose ONE adjective. Focus on each noun at a time and ask them to decide which adjective tells the reader what you need them to know. Is it more important that they know the dinosaur is big, heavy or green?

Your pupils might find it helpful to see other examples of adjectives to practise identifying and dealing with them. Activity B on page 43 has several examples that you could share with your class.

2. Stating the obvious

This happens when your pupils haven't thought about what they are describing or why. They've heard that adjectives are a good way to improve their writing and so start sticking them in unnecessarily. For example:

The orange, stripy tiger prowled through the jungle, looking for something to eat.
The bonfire was hot.
The ice cream was freezing cold.

None of this description tells the reader anything new; in fact, it just spells out assumptions that they would probably have made. Ice cream generally is cold, old ladies tend to have wrinkled skin and elephants are normally big and grey. Unnecessary description distracts the reader from the story. Ask your pupils to go back and look at their work, asking themselves the question: 'Does my reader already know this?'

3. Swallowed the thesaurus

We all want our pupils to use ambitious and challenging vocabulary. However, by pushing this too hard, we can end up with our pupils thinking that the longer the word, the better the writing, when in fact, nine times out of ten, the opposite is true. We often hear pupils say, 'I need a better word for small!' and my answer is always the same: 'Why? What's wrong with using small?'

This approach can lead to your pupils spending their lesson time poring over the thesaurus for a 'better word', and while a thesaurus does offer you groups of words with a similar meaning, it doesn't explain the subtle differences in meaning. This can lead to writing like this:

James raced across the verdant pitch, his heart beating furiously in his chest. His teammates were shouting instructions, but he couldn't apprehend them over the approbation from the parents on the side-lines. They were going to be victorious. His team had played the Heartland Eagles every Saturday for six weeks, and on each dispiriting occasion they had been overcome. Despite the abounding rain, he adroitly dribbled the ball; his expeditious footsteps were as agile as a feather, as he darted between the defenders. With the goal in sight, he gave the ball a vigorous kick and eyeballed it as it shot neatly into the top left corner.

Without a thesaurus, this piece of writing might have looked something like this:

James raced across the pitch, his heart beating furiously in his chest. His teammates were shouting instructions, but he couldn't hear them over the cheers from the parents on the side-lines. They were going to win. His team had played the Heartland Eagles every Saturday for six weeks and every time they had lost. He skilfully dribbled the ball, his footsteps as light as a feather, darting between the defenders. With the goal in sight, he gave the ball a hard kick and watched as it shot neatly into the top left corner.

The solution? Get rid of the thesaurus and get rid of references to 'wow words'. In most cases, the words that your pupils would naturally use are the ones that will make the writing sound more authentic and readable.

4. Wannabe Dickens

This is particularly common in upper Key Stage 2 and lower Key Stage 3. It's your able writer who has moved on from the thesaurus but is still holding onto the idea that the more description they include, the better the writing will be. Their writing probably reads just fine and their use of grammar and punctuation is accurate, but they are still writing like an able Year 6 writer, rather than like a writer. Their work might be so heavy with description that it reads more like poetry and prose. It looks a bit like this:

> **Sophia's eyes glistened like diamonds pouring from a treasure chest. She looked up at the fluorescent sky; the light was dancing, sprite-like as the sun slowly retreated to the horizon. The clouds smiled down on her knowingly as she made her way over the soft, undulating sand. The chirping sounds of the birds carried through the soft, summer breeze and a feeling of peace swept over her, like the waves lapping on the shore.**

While there's nothing technically wrong with this piece of writing, it is quite jarring for the reader; the description distracts the reader from the plot, making it harder to follow. A lot of capable young writers will go through a stage of writing like this, keen to show off their sophisticated use of language. Once again, it comes back to what the purpose of the description is – what does the reader need to know? Everything comes back to readability; good writing is easy to read.

It's time to challenge this writer to move away from descriptive writing. Can they write a clear and concise science report? Can they write a story that uses flashbacks? Can they use humour or irony in their writing? Could they perhaps write a narrative from the perspective of two different characters? Finding new ways to challenge their writing and move them on will keep them on their toes and hopefully take their attention away from description – at least for a while!

Summary

There is no such thing as a powerful adjective (or adverb). Adjectives modify nouns (adverbs modify verbs) and they make them as powerful, as weak, as big, as small, as luminescent or as antidisestablishmentarian as you want them to be. Teach your pupils to think about the purpose of their descriptions and the impact that they have on the reader.

Where next?

The resources below should help you to address some of these common errors with your class. In the next chapter, we will look at different ways to build descriptions and explore how choosing the right noun or verb can be more effective than relying on adjectives and adverbs.

Resources and modelled texts

Activity A: What's the point?

This short activity helps children to focus on the purpose of their description – what it is that they are trying to communicate. It can be modified for different word classes and is suitable for all year groups.

Start by writing up the following sentence:

Maria opened the door to her _____, _____ car.

Then ask your class to jot down two adjectives that they might choose if they wanted the reader to think that:

- Maria is a rich and arrogant businesswoman.
- Maria is a gentle old lady.
- Maria is neither rich nor poor but she is obsessed with her image.
- Maria is an undercover police officer trying to go unnoticed.

Remember: We don't want makes or models of cars. We want adjectives.

You can extend this activity by including an adverb, e.g. Maria hurriedly opened the door to her sleek, expensive car.

Maria_____ opened the door to her _____, _____ car.

Once again, your pupils will need to think carefully about their choice of adverb. How does the reader's perception of Maria change if she opens the door cautiously? What might the reader infer if Maria opens the door to her car silently? Have these discussions with your class – let them explore how, by just changing one or two words, they can alter their reader's perception of Maria.

Activity B: Adjective pile-up

Uh oh – we have a severe case of adjective pile-up! Read the sentences and then rewrite them with one adjective for each noun. Choose the adjective that you think makes the most sense in the context of the sentence.

1. The big, heavy, green dinosaurs trampled over the hot, dusty, red ground and let out a loud, scary roar.

Rewrite the sentence here: _____.

2. The happy, old, ginger cat yawned as it stretched out on the big, blue, fluffy mat.

Rewrite the sentence here: _____.

3. Every Saturday my lovely, kind, generous dad takes me to the sweet shop to buy some tasty, delicious, yummy chocolate.

Rewrite the sentence here: _____.

4. The happy, little children were playing in the big, green, lush park.

Rewrite the sentence here: _____.

5. As Mia trudged through the heavy, torrential, endless rain, she regretted leaving her big, red and white umbrella at home.

Rewrite the sentence here: _____.

6. The big, old, mysterious house stood on top of the tall, scary hill.

Rewrite the sentence here: _____.

Activity C: Swallowed a thesaurus

Have a look at this piece of writing and circle any words that you don't understand. Then use a dictionary to look up what they mean. Next, rewrite this passage, focusing on being clear and using meaningful description that the reader can understand.

> **James raced across the verdant pitch, his heart beating furiously in his chest. His teammates were shouting instructions, but he couldn't apprehend them over the approbation from the parents on the side-lines. They were going to be victorious. His team had played the Heartland Eagles every Saturday for six weeks and on each dispiriting occasion, they had been overcome. Despite the abounding rain, he adroitly dribbled the ball; his expeditious footsteps were as agile as a feather, as he darted between the defenders. With the goal in sight, he gave the ball a vigorous kick and eyeballed it as it shot neatly into the top left corner.**

Modelled writing

Text 1: Sara's bad day

Use this text to demonstrate how sparingly writers use adjectives. It also shows how adjectives do not need to be elaborate to have an impact; in fact, often, less is more. Ask pupils to read the text and highlight all the nouns, verbs and adverbs in different colours. Then use the discussion questions to review the text as a class.

Sara's bad day

Sara stretched her arms above her head and let out a loud yawn. It had been a long day. It had started badly: her train was cancelled, she had spilt hot coffee on herself and had been caught in torrential rain without an umbrella. She had arrived late to her morning meeting, interrupting her boss, who was in the middle of a big presentation. As she had arrived late, she felt it necessary to work through her lunch break, devouring a soggy sandwich at her desk while responding to emails, ignoring her colleague's cheerful chatter that was echoing up from the canteen. It was now 3.00 pm and Sara was tired, hungry and still smelt faintly of coffee, despite her attempts to dry her outfit under the hand dryer in the toilet.

She absentmindedly rolled a piece of sticky tack between her thumb and forefinger and thought about what she was going to have for dinner. It was Wednesday, which was the night her housemate worked late; it was also Sara's favourite evening of the week. With the flat to herself, she could watch whatever she wanted on the TV. She decided at that moment that she was going to treat herself to a takeaway: Mexican food maybe, or even sushi. With thoughts of a relaxing evening ahead, Sara turned back to her computer, smiling to herself. Her terrible day was nearly over.

Discussion questions:

- How many adjectives did you find?
- How many nouns did you find?
- How many adverbs did you find?
- What do you notice about the number of nouns vs. the number of adjectives?
- Look at the adjectives that the author has chosen: why do you think they chose to describe these parts of the text? What effect does it have on the reader?
- Look at the writer's choice of adjectives – loud, hot, big. Would these sentences be better if they had used deafening, scorching or enormous? How would using more elaborate adjectives change the sentence?

Text 2: The jungle

Use this text to model cutting out unnecessary descriptive language. Start by reading it as a class and asking your pupils to highlight any superfluous words, encouraging them to explain why. Then rewrite the text as a class, taking suggestions from the pupils about what needs to be changed.

The jungle

The tall, green trees towered over me like shiny skyscrapers; the blue sky could no longer be seen. Tentatively, I stepped forward, the dry branches cracking under my feet. There was no one around but the jungle was filled with a cacophony of sound. A colourful bird squawked from a branch; a brown, furry monkey chattered as it swung through the trees; the heavy steps of the big, grey elephant echoed as it stomped through the leaves. The dark green backdrop of the jungle was decorated with a rainbow of colours from bright flowers, colourful feathers and luminous insects. My initial fear subsided and I continued walking, growing in confidence with each step. The sun was shining through the canopy of leaves, leaving a dappled pattern on the ground. My mood began to lift; that is when it happened. If only I had looked where I was going. If only I had listened out for the clues: the rustle of the dry leaves, the wriggling in the corner of my eye or the gentle hissing sound approaching…

Discussion questions:

- Which adjectives do you think enhance the description? Which ones tell us something that we don't already know?
- Are there any adjectives that are distracting for the reader? Which ones?
- What other descriptive techniques can you spot in this text? Are they effective?
- If you were going to rewrite this paragraph, what would you change?

Chapter 5
Precision engineering: Selecting the right nouns and verbs

Having spent a chapter explaining the pitfalls of teaching descriptive writing, let's explore some solutions. In the last chapter, we argued against encouraging your pupils to pepper their writing with needless adjectives and adverbs. In order to keep their sentences succinct and efficient, you want to encourage them instead to focus on the nouns and verbs that they use, especially when it comes to the subject and the main verb of their sentence. If they make these as precise as possible, it will make a significant difference to their writing.

In this chapter, we will explore the idea that selecting precise nouns and verbs will make unnecessary adjectives and adverbs obsolete. As you'll see in the examples in this chapter, if your pupils choose precise nouns and verbs, their writing will be more accurate and succinct. By reducing unnecessary adjectives, you free up space in the sentence for the description that matters. This chapter builds on the principles outlined in Chapter 3: Less is more: Being succinct – so, if you've just dipped into the book, you may find it helpful to head there first.

Why it matters

Let's start with the example of a pleasingly succinct sentence that we used in Chapter 3:

> **Unperturbed by either of his previous defeats, the King returned the following spring and successfully besieged the enemy capital.**

Now, did we not all agree that we would like to see our pupils writing like this? This sentence contains three adjectives (previous, following, enemy) and one adverb (successfully). None of these are rich, descriptive words but are largely functional and cohesive in nature. They simply explain the relationships between the elements in the sentence and the order in which things happened. The richness of this sentence is found in its four nouns (defeats, King, spring, capital) and three verbs (unperturbed, returned, besieged).

Nouns and verbs form the core of any sentence. Unless it's a gerund (*a verb phrase functioning as a noun, e.g. reading books is great fun*), the subject of a sentence will usually be a noun, a noun phrase or a pronoun. The main verb will either be a single verb or several verbs that form a verb phrase (*e.g. I have been expecting you, Mr Bond*). Nouns and verbs are like the main dish when you're having a curry. The other words in the sentence (the prepositions, adverbs, adjectives, conjunctions, etc.) are the rice, naan, onion bhajis and vegetable side dishes. You wouldn't want to be without them but, if you've chosen the wrong main course, they won't make a good meal on their own!

How to do it

Precise nouns

What do we mean by precise nouns? It means choosing a noun that has the description 'built in'. For example, instead of telling you that we played a game, I tell you that we played Monopoly; the new car that my friend bought is actually a hatchback; the woman did not order beef, she ordered steak. Precise nouns tell the reader more and take away the need for additional description.

Have a look at this in action:

The white and black spotted dog was running across the field.

If I use a precise noun, that sentence reads like this:

A Dalmatian was running across the field.

By choosing the word 'Dalmatian', the reader automatically pictures a white and black spotted dog, which means that I can shorten my sentence, making that sentence more succinct. Precise nouns suggest accuracy and attention to detail on behalf of the writer.

Precise verbs

Often, we ask pupils to focus on 'ambitious verbs' or 'powerful verbs' when actually it is precise verbs that will improve their writing. Like precise nouns, precise verbs tell the reader exactly what the character is doing and how they are doing it.

Let's look at another example.

I could write:

The mean, unkind person hit him hard in the face with his clenched fist.

If I choose precise nouns and verbs, then the sentence becomes:

The bully punched him.

These two sentences have the same meaning. The reader assumes that a punch is delivered with a clenched fist. And, although it is possible to punch someone on any part of their body, simply saying that 'he punched him' will make most people imagine that it's a punch to the face.

If you tell me that someone is a bully, you don't need to tell me that they are mean and unkind. Once again, one sentence is long and clumsy but the other is short and efficient.

At this point, we'd like to raise the issue of vocabulary. Inevitably, your pupils' ability to identify precise nouns and verbs is capped by their vocabulary. The English language is a funny one in many ways. We have only one word for 'love' and yet we have a separate word for a 'portcullis' when talking about a specific type of gate on a type of building that we haven't used for hundreds of years. Vocabulary-building should be a key pillar of your English lesson – not just introducing your pupils to new vocabulary but exploring morphology: unpicking language, looking at root words and playing around with suffixes and prefixes. Teaching vocabulary is a whole other book in itself, and thankfully one that other people have written. We highly recommend *Closing the Vocabulary Gap* by Alex Quigley (2018) and *Vocabulary Ninja: Activities to unlock a world of words* by Andrew Jennings (2019).

Now, back to modifiers.

Adding other modifiers

Once your pupils have started using precise nouns and verbs, they might be happy to enjoy their new succinct writing style, or they might want to focus on modifying other parts of the sentence. Let's have a look at another example:

If we didn't give a damn about precise verbs and nouns, we might end up with a clunky sentence like this:

> **A person who plans buildings drew a picture of his idea for a new one: it was really tall, modern and thin.**

You can probably see where we're going with this. Most of us would express the same idea like this:

> **The architect designed a skyscraper.**

The precise nouns and verb enable us to focus on what it is that we want the reader to know about the architect and the skyscraper. We have freed up room in our sentence for other modifiers that provide additional meaning.

For example, I might want the reader to know that:

> **The complacent architect designed a dodgy skyscraper.**
> **The imaginative architect designed an unusual skyscraper.**
> **The Roman architect designed a skyscraper, or so it would have seemed to his contemporaries.**

In these examples, the selection of modifiers has significantly changed the reader's perception of the character.

Size doesn't matter

It's important to emphasise that this has nothing to do with the length of words. Our mission here is not to encourage children to use longer and more 'fancy' nouns or verbs for the sake of it. Of course, if your character is going to throw their enemy out of the window, there is no more succinct verb to use than 'defenestrate'. Very often, however, we're looking for something much more subtle. Many of the most precise verbs that we use are actually very short: *browse, prowl, snatch, glance, trace, earn, crave, delve, cope, slide, claim, breach*. The same is true of nouns, especially abstract ones.

Try to avoid giving your pupils the idea that you are looking to reward long and unusual words. Often, what matters is choosing the right everyday word for the job. 'The guards scoured the cellar' is a better sentence than 'the defenders interrogated the substructure', for example.

Common verbs and phrasal verbs

To be, *to have*, *to go*, *to get* and *to do* are five of the most common verbs in the English language. Because they have been used so often over so many years, they have undergone the most change and evolution. This is why their past tense forms are so irregular (*I was*, *I had*, *I went*, *I got*, *I did*), which often makes them hard to spot. If you ask most Key Stage 2 children to find the verbs in a passage, they'll all be able to spot 'rematerialised' or 'dismembered', but spotting 'had', 'done', 'gone', 'got' or 'is', for example, can often present more of a challenge. These five verbs are important ones for you to look out for, however, as they are often overused in clumsy, inefficient sentences. Moreover, they are often the verbs that can most easily be replaced with a more precise alternative to bring the sentence to life. The same is true of other very common verbs: *to say*, *to make*, *to come*, *to see*, *to take*, *to move*, *to put*, *to think*, etc.

Spoken English is full of *phrasal verbs*: common verbs that are modified in a very specific way by the addition of a preposition. Here are some examples:

go on, go out, go over, go through, go in

do up, do over, do in, do down, do away

get on, get over, get up, get away, get in

The meaning of these verbs is completely altered by the preposition that follows them, and we use phrasal verbs all the time. They often work less effectively when we're writing (partly because they can become a lot more ambiguous when they're written down) and you might want to encourage your pupils to come up with alternatives where possible.

It's important to emphasise that we are not saying that your pupils should never use common or phrasal verbs in their writing – just that they should avoid overreliance on them, and that it is a good idea to teach them about the alternatives at their disposal.

Do you ALWAYS need a precise noun or verb?

Writing is about making decisions. As teachers, our job is to provide our pupils with a selection of tools and techniques to use and give them plenty of opportunities to practise using them. In time, they will learn to judge when precise nouns are most effective, but to start with a useful rule of thumb is only to use a precise noun or verb if you want to draw attention to a particular part of the sentence. Have a look at this sentence:

Elika winced; she had stubbed her hallux.

In this moment, we probably want the reader to empathise with Elika's discomfort. Instead, your reader's attention is going to be diverted by the needlessly specific and anatomical term that you have used for 'big toe'.

Similarly, in the modelled text, 'Monday' on page 53, the final sentence is: 'What difference would one cup of coffee make?' If you were being particularly zealous with your use of precise nouns, then 'cup of coffee' could be 'cappuccino' or 'latte', for example.

What difference would one cappuccino make?

In such a short sentence, the word cappuccino distracts from the main point, which is that Joseph decides it's worth being late to work for the sake of a cup of coffee from his favourite cafe. Cappuccino wouldn't be incorrect, but it changes the focus of the sentence, and will needlessly summon all of the reader's assumptions about someone who chooses a cappuccino over any other kind of coffee.

Many of these decisions therefore come down to how the sentence *sounds*, and developing the ear to judge that takes years of reading and writing. So, in the meantime, ask your pupils to focus on which nouns and verbs are important and focus on making those as precise and accurate as possible.

Non-fiction

Often, when we teach writing in primary school, we teach children to write fiction. When we do teach non-fiction writing, we teach it in a specific unit, e.g. writing a newspaper article or a review. The vast majority of the writing that your pupils will do as an adult will be non-fiction – letters of application, reports, summaries and presentations. In these contexts, precision matters, and being selective with your verb and noun choices is an effective way of achieving this. We've all sat through waffle-filled and unclear presentations, or read letters of application that are two pages too long; being precise with your word choices is often more important when writing non-fiction than fiction.

While we are not big believers in the idea that education should only be about preparing children for the world of work, it would seem prudent to dedicate a bit more of our curriculum time to teaching children how to write clearly and effectively in non-fiction contexts. At this point, you may roll your eyes – the curriculum is jam-packed as it is, without more helpful suggestions about what you could be teaching, but it can often be done through other subjects rather than taking up more of your English lesson. Written work in science and humanities provides a great opportunity to practise this skill, especially as remembering and using key vocabulary is such an important part of those subjects.

We know that providing opportunities for pupils to retrieve information from their working memory and apply it is the way to help them to remember it in the long term. After teaching a new concept, ask your pupils to write a short and clear explanation of the concept. You might even decide to give them a word limit to force them to really think about their noun and verb choices, e.g. 'In 50 words, can you explain the concept of hydraulic action?' As always, you will need to have modelled this a few times, including the process of editing a long-winded explanation into a short, concise one. There is a modelled text of this task in the resources section that you could use.

Summary

People wrongly assume that the descriptive power of sentences is found in its adjectives and adverbs. While they can be a useful addition in certain circumstances, they are no substitute for choosing the correct nouns and verbs to begin with. You need to encourage your children to decide exactly who or what their sentence is about and then decide exactly what that person or object is doing, being or experiencing. If they can find the right nouns and verbs to express these ideas, their sentence will probably be a good one.

Where next?

You can now have a look at the resources and modelled text section for this chapter or head to the next chapter on page 59. Having unpacked what we mean by effective description, the next few chapters explore the impact that varying the word order can have on your pupils' sentences.

Resources and modelled texts

Generating precise nouns

A simple exercise for getting pupils used to generating precise nouns:

General	Precise
dog	Dalmatian
bird	
car	
relative	
tool	
shoe	
flower	
building	

The first has been done as an example. Once they are comfortable with this, move your pupils onto applying this skill to an extended piece of writing. The modelled text 'Monday' is perfect for this.

Phrasal verbs

Here is a list of common phrasal verbs. Share these with your pupils and see whether they can come up with slightly more precise alternatives. The first has been done as an example:

Go on – *continue*

Do up –

Get over –

Find out –

Make up –

Get up –

See through –

Clear up –

Fall out –

Take on –

Work out –

Put up –

Go away –

Put down –

Bring up –

Take away –

Modelled writing

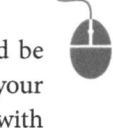

Read these extracts with your class and discuss which nouns, adjectives or verbs could be replaced with more precise equivalents. Then, either as a class or individually, challenge your pupils to rewrite the modelled texts, replacing the general nouns, adjectives and verbs with precise ones.

Monday

> Joseph walked quickly down the narrow side road. He looked at his watch and sighed; he was late for work again. With the wet weather showing no sign of improving, he quickly took his umbrella from his coat pocket and opened it above his head. He continued along the road; the cars drove past quickly, splashing the water up onto the pavement. Why were Mondays like this? Transport was always delayed, the weather was always miserable and people walked into work with grumpy expressions on their faces. At the end of the alley, at the point where it met the main road, was a coffee shop. Joseph's favourite coffee shop. The warm coloured lights were as inviting as the smell of roasted coffee beans coming out of the windows. Joseph looked at his watch again. He was already late. What difference would a cup of coffee make?

For reference, here is one way in which you could alter this text to include precise nouns and verbs:

Joseph **marched** down the **alleyway**. He looked at his watch and sighed; he was late for work again. With the **rain** showing no sign of improving, he **grabbed** his umbrella from his coat pocket and opened it above his head. He continued along the **alley**; the cars **sped past**, **spraying water** onto the pavement. **The trains** were always delayed, the weather was always miserable and **everyone trudged** to work with a **scowl** on their face. **On the corner of the alley** was **Carlo's Café**. Joseph's favourite coffee shop. The **warm glow** was as inviting as the smell of roasted coffee beans **pouring** out of the window. Joseph **glanced** at his watch again. He was already late. What difference would a cup of coffee make?

A walk in the park

The woman picked up her pace to keep up with the spotty dog who was running quickly through the park. He pulled jerkily on the lead, eager to go and explore everything the park had to offer. There was the large patch of grass to play on, the soil with the flowers sitting in a row to dig in and, best of all, the large expanse of water. He really liked the large expanse of water and longed to go and play in it. The woman was breathing quickly as she struggled to keep up with him. He was a much quicker runner than her. He slowed his pace down from a fast run to a slow one so she could get her breath back. He looked around the park. The tree with all the glossy conkers on looked very appealing; all the leaves had dropped off and were now on the ground just asking to be run around in. There were some small children who were having fun in the leaves and throwing them at each other. Once he was sure that the woman had got her breath back, he ran quickly towards the big tree.

Once again, here is one way in which you could alter this text to include precise nouns and verbs:

The woman picked up her pace to keep up with the spotty dog who was **tearing** through the park. He **yanked** on the lead, eager to go and explore everything the park had to offer. There was the **field** to play on, the soil with the flowerbed to dig in and, best of all, the lake. He really liked the lake and longed to go and play in it. The woman was **breathless** as she struggled to keep up with him. He was much **faster** than her. He slowed his pace down from a **run** to a **jog** so she could get her breath back. He looked around the park. The **horse chestnut tree** with all the glossy conkers on looked very appealing; all the leaves had **fallen to the** ground just asking to be run around in. There were some small children who were **playing** in the leaves and throwing them at each other. Once he was sure that the woman had got her breath back, he **sprinted** towards the big tree.

Hydraulic action: Explanation text

Read Version 1 as a class – and then challenge your pupils to rewrite the explanation using no more than 50 words. Alternatively, you might want to give them both versions and ask them to compare them, using the following questions as a starting point for your discussion:

- Which version do you find easiest to understand?
- Which one is clearer?
- Which nouns and verbs have changed and to what effect?
- Are there any nouns or verbs that you would change in Version 2 to improve it further?

Version 1
Hydraulic action is a type of coastal erosion. It is when the water hits the rocks, which then pushes the air into cracks in the rocks. The air in the cracks creates pressure and sometimes it can cause the rock to split or parts to splinter off. If this happens repeatedly, then it can cause cracks in the rocks to expand into caves that you sometimes see on a cliff.

Version 2
Hydraulic action occurs when the force of the waves pushes air into the cracks of a cliff face. The air exerts pressure on the surrounding rock, causing it to split or splinter. Over time, this process can cause cracks to expand into caves in the cliff face.

Rainforest descriptions

Finally, here are two more pieces of descriptive writing to discuss with your pupils. Again, encourage them to think as much about the nouns and verbs involved as the adjectives and adverbs:

Into the rainforest

Struck by awe and wonder, I stepped forward into the foliage. Here and there, sunbeams cut through occasional gaps in the trees high above: wraithlike blades of otherworldly light thrust into the forest floor. My eyes had now fully adapted to this ethereal dimness and yet, as I beheld the scene before me, I could still scarcely process the rich tapestry of colours and textures woven by the myriad life of the rainforest. The feel of the light, misty rain on my skin was refreshing, given the humid warmth of my surroundings. The air was thick and close but it carried a subtle and complex perfume: an ever-changing blend of a thousand exotic flowers.

I was flanked on either side by thick Aphelandra shrubs. At first they appeared to be a homogenous mass of green but, on closer inspection, I could see all the wonder of nature etched on the plants in intricate detail. Beads of moisture balanced delicately on the edges of their sharp, waxy leaves; they caught the narrow shafts of sunlight and illuminated the web-like patterns formed by the plant's complex network of veins.

Moments later, my attention was snatched suddenly from what lay immediately beside me by a strange, high-pitched noise high in the trees. The call of a bird, I assumed, or perhaps some sort of climbing mammal. I listened closely and, as the sound abated, I started to pay close attention to everything else I could hear: the stridulating of the crickets, the chirruping of the tree frogs and the intermittent cheeping of birds all contributed to the rainforest's remarkable natural choir.

As I revelled in those thoughts, a macaw leaped forth from a branch high in the canopy and soared majestically through the relatively open space of the understorey. I was captivated both by the grace of its movement and by the bright colours of its plumage: its body was a brilliant shade of crimson and its wings were striped in yellow and blue. Above my head, a furry sloth slowly raised its head and watched the gliding bird uncertainly, its beady black eyes following the bird's path intently for a moment before losing interest.

Ruins of an ancient city

I step gingerly up the wide, uneven steps. They dip in the middle, the silvery rock apparently worn down over centuries by the relentless footfall of ancient people. Vines and creepers encroach on the stairs from the sides: their gradual invasion a natural reminder that whoever was here once is here no more – long gone now; long forgotten; long dead.

I emerge into a cobbled courtyard surrounded by imposing buildings, all the same silvery grey as the stairs I've just ascended. For a moment, I fancy that I can see movement at one of the windows but I know that's impossible. An eerie silence permeates the city as if the whole world were paying its respects to the fallen greatness of an extinct civilisation. At my feet, ancient columns and fragments litter the floor – clues from the past unreadable to me but perhaps of interest to archaeologists. In the centre of the courtyard stands an old, weathered statue. Perhaps this is a great ruler from the city's past or even a god whom its people once worshipped. There is no one left to ask. Its narrow eyes stare at me, as if judging me for trespassing.

Streets lined with similar though smaller buildings snake off this central courtyard in every direction. At the far end of the city, a formidable pyramid dominates the former settlement, crowned by a temple just visible through the ghostly mist that shrouds its summit. As I resolve to explore the pyramid and begin to set off in its direction, I am stopped in my tracks by a noise – not close but not far away. It sounds like a metallic object crashing to the floor. Perhaps I'm not alone after all…

Chapter 6
Front and back:
Varying word order

There is a very famous Morecambe and Wise sketch from the 1970s in which Eric Morecambe attempts to play a Grieg piano concerto, but does so dreadfully. Afterwards, having been told that he was playing 'all the wrong notes', Morecambe responds: 'I'm playing all the right notes – but not necessarily in the right order.' The joke, of course, is that the order in which the notes are played is absolutely fundamental to our concept of playing 'the right notes'. This chapter deals with the most basic issue of all when it comes to arranging our words: the order of words within a sentence. As Morecambe and Wise's joke reminds us, this can be of equal importance to choosing the right words in the first place.

Why it matters

Word order is much, much more complicated than we sometimes think. Even if you only have three words, there are six possible ways in which to arrange them:

Rob is Scottish
Rob Scottish is
Scottish is Rob
Scottish Rob is
Is Rob Scottish
Is Scottish Rob

The first of these is a grammatically recognisable and conventional sentence. If your aim is to inform someone of Rob's nationality, this is clearly the most elegant way to do it. The second, third and fourth iterations sound like Yoda from *Star Wars* and, if delivered with the right intonation, could probably be understood. The fifth option could be a question if it ended with a question mark and the sixth option, while essentially devoid of sense, could actually be uttered by someone with limited English and be just about understood. Here, there is an important point to make about children with English as an additional language. They can make surprising mistakes in word order that aren't always easy to explain, especially if the grammatical conventions of their first language are radically different from those of English. The sixth option could also be the start of a question if you had more than one friend called Rob, one of whom was habitually identified by his Scottishness: 'Is Scottish Rob coming tonight?' However, we're not really sure how respectful this would be, so we'll move swiftly on!

Most sentences, of course, are considerably longer than three words and, with each extra word that you add, the number of possible arrangements gets exponentially larger – 24 for four words, 120 for five words and so on. If a sentence has 11 different words, there are almost 40 million possible combinations in which its words can be arranged. If a sentence has 16 different words, there are over 20 trillion combinations. It's a miracle that we so often agree on one appropriate arrangement. What's even more common with longer sentences is that there are a few different combinations that would be grammatically acceptable, and we have to choose one. For example:

> **I wear a coat when I'm going to school if it's raining.**
> **I wear a coat if it's raining when I'm going to school.**
> **If it's raining when I'm going to school, I wear a coat.**
> **If it's raining, I wear a coat when I'm going to school.**
> **When I'm going to school, I wear a coat if it's raining.**
> **When I'm going to school, if it's raining, I wear a coat.**

Without any additional context, there is very little difference in sense or emphasis between these six sentences – they mean almost exactly the same thing. You can pretty much take your pick and perhaps choose an order that makes the sentence sound as distinct as possible from the ones before and after it. However, the way in which we rearrange sentences can sometimes subtly alter the way in which we perceive it, especially if the subject matter is more sensitive than the matter of wearing a coat to school:

> **The money needs to be repaid; it would be really helpful if it could be transferred in two instalments.**
> **It would be helpful if the money could be repaid; it really needs to be transferred in two instalments.**

These sentences contain exactly the same words and they are conveying the same basic message but there are all sorts of differences in nuance. The first clause of the first sentence is much more direct than the first clause of the second sentence and suggests a different level of impatience with the person being addressed. Haven't we all agonised over the wording of these sorts of sentences at some point? The way in which we arrange the words in our sentences can sometimes seem like the most important issue in the world.

How to do it

This is, by necessity, a fairly grammar-heavy chapter. If this fills you with trepidation, we encourage you to read *The Grammar Book*. Many of your fears are more easily overcome than you may think! However, even in this book, we promise not to leave anyone behind – any complicated grammar terminology will be clearly and simply explained as we go. To start with, we need to ensure that we're happy with the difference between a *phrase* and a *clause*, as these two words are indispensable when discussing the ways in which sentences can be reorganised.

Phrases

A *phrase* is any group of words that stands as a distinct item in a sentence. For example, in the sentence 'Sylvia drives a big, red combine harvester', we can pick out the thing that Sylvia drives, which is a 'big, red combine harvester' and we can identify that these four words are identifying a single object. They are behaving like a noun (you could replace them all with the word 'tractor' and the grammar of the sentence would still work in the same way). So, in this sentence, 'big, red combine harvester' is a *noun phrase*. A phrase that stands in for a single verb (e.g. the words 'will have been going' in the sentence '*The Archers* will have been going for three-quarters of a century when it celebrates its 75th anniversary in 2026') is a *verb phrase*. You can also have phrases that stand in for prepositions (prepositional phrases), adjectives (adjectival phrases) or adverbs (adverbial phrases). Chapter 12 of *The Grammar Book* provides more information about the different types of phrase. To understand what phrases are, your pupils will need to have a solid understanding of different types of word class, so you need to keep rehearsing these with them.

Clauses

A *clause* is a part of a sentence that contains its own subject and predicate (including a main verb). In grammar terminology, a simple sentence is a sentence with one 'main' clause:

The cat sat on the mat.

'The cat' is the only subject of the sentence and 'sat' is the only main verb.

However, some sentences (called *complex sentences*) contain a main clause and one or more *subordinate clauses* (or *dependent clauses*). A dependent clause is one that relies on the main clause in order to make sense. For example:

When the sun went down, the cat sat on the mat.

The first clause, 'when the sun went down', contains a subject ('the sun') and a main verb ('went') but it only makes sense when you read on to the main clause.

Some sentences, known as *compound sentences*, contain more than one main clause:

The cat sat on the mat and the dog sat on the chair.

In this example, the two clauses are of equal importance. Each would make sense on its own and they have been linked in this case by 'and', which is one of the seven coordinating conjunctions that can be remembered using the acronym FANBOYS (for, and, nor, but, or, yet, so). Main clauses can also be linked with a semicolon (;) or a dash (–) but not with a comma.

The dreaded fronted adverbial

Now that we've established what we mean when we talk about phrases and clauses, we're ready to look at some of the specific ways in which sentences can be rearranged. Where better to start than with the poster boy for people's fears about grammar – the dreaded fronted adverbial? It's far from clear why this has become such a red rag to the anti-grammar bulls in recent years, given what a simple concept it is. If you're unsure, let's just make it clear how simple it really is:

I play football on Saturdays.

This sentence contains a subject ('I'), a verb ('play') and an object ('football') and then it is finished off with an adverbial ('on Saturdays'). What makes that last phrase an adverbial? Well, because it is behaving as an adverb and modifying the verb 'play'. Adverbs can tell us when, where, why or how the action denoted by the verb is carried out. In this case, the phrase 'on Saturdays' tells us when the playing happens. So, how do I make my adverbial phrase into a *fronted adverbial*? Right, well this is the really technical bit, so concentrate carefully. A fronted adverbial is an adverbial (OK?) that goes (get ready for it) at the front:

On Saturdays, I play football.

Is the sentence any better because the adverbial is at the front? Probably not. Is this a simple and useful trick that you can teach children in order to rearrange some of their sentences and add a bit of variety? Yes, of course. Here are a few other examples. In some cases, the adverbial is a single word (an adverb), in some cases it is an adverbial phrase (as in the example above) and in some cases it is an adverbial clause. The only other detail to point out is that when the adverbial is fronted, it tends to be followed by a comma. This is not necessary when the adverbial comes at the end of the sentence.

You can go and play when you've finished your dinner.
When you've finished your dinner, you can go and play.

The defender took the free kick quickly.
Quickly, the defender took the free kick.

We ate dinner at Grandma's flat.
At Grandma's flat, we ate dinner.

I awoke suddenly.
Suddenly, I awoke.

She walked into the road without looking.
Without looking, she walked into the road.

I can't see that happening in all honesty.
In all honesty, I can't see that happening.

Embedding

Another simple way in which your pupils can reorganise their sentences is by embedding elements of them – that is to say, they can be placed in the middle of your sentence with two commas either side. Almost any sort of clause or phrase (including adverbials) can be embedded in the right context – usually either in between the subject and the main verb or between the main verb and the rest of the predicate:

New pupils, often a little shy, can take a while to adapt.   *Embedded adjectival phrase*
She realised, when it was over, that it could have been   *Embedded adverbial clause*
a lot worse.

His opponent, humiliated, left the field silently. *Embedded verb/adjective*

Embedding is a very simple concept to teach because it contains the word 'bed' and there is a very useful analogy here. Imagine a mattress with a fitted sheet on it and then another sheet between the sleeper and the duvet. The mattress and the duvet represent the main clause of the sentence. The two sheets represent the commas and the sleeper represents the embedded word, phrase or clause.

Relative clauses

Just as adverbials provide the reader with more information or specification about the main verb in a sentence, relative clauses provide them with more information or specification about the subject or the object. They are often embedded, particularly when being used to describe the subject of the sentence, and they generally begin with a relative pronoun (who, whom, whose, which, where, when):

My brother, <u>who has never enjoyed confrontation</u>, has had a dispute with his neighbour.
I think that car, <u>which hasn't moved for two months</u>, might have been abandoned.
I gave both my tickets to Bethan, <u>whose sister has always wanted to go</u>.
I think it must have happened during the winter of 2007, <u>when we had quite a lot of snow</u>.

In Chapter 3, we looked at the importance of being succinct. A great way to do this is to take the information from one sentence and combine it with another one to create one slightly more efficient sentence – relative clauses are a great way in which to do this.

Participle clauses

Participle clauses are an incredibly useful tool for your pupils to have at their disposal, both for varying their sentence structures and for ensuring succinctness. They are a specific type of adverbial (or sometimes adjectival) clause that begins with the past or present participle form of a verb (don't panic – that often just means a verb ending in -ed or -ing). They can be placed at the beginning or the end of a sentence, or embedded within it:

<u>Angered by the performance of his team the previous week</u>, the manager made several changes to the starting XI.
<u>Realising that the summit was further than she thought</u>, Zara decided to pitch her tent and continue the climb in the morning.
Several of the children in Archie's class, <u>hoping to make him feel better while his mum was in hospital</u>, decided to make him a card.
Professor Pinceau could hardly believe that he was actually holding the original canvas, <u>painted by Monet himself well over a century ago</u>.

Once your pupils are used to using participle clauses in their writing, it's worth pointing out that many participle clauses can actually be *negated* – that is to say, the verb at the head of the clause can be prefixed with *un-, in-, dis-*, etc. This can be a very effective way in which to pack a lot of information into a single sentence:

<u>Unconcerned for his own safety</u>, he marched back into the burning building.
<u>Displeasing his coach but delighting the crowds</u>, the gymnast attempted a very risky move.

And, of course, our old favourite:

<u>Unperturbed by his previous defeats</u>, the King returned the following spring and successfully besieged the enemy capital.

'Despite' and other useful words for rearranging sentences

Generally speaking, we'd avoid advocating the use of any particular pieces of vocabulary. However, the word 'despite' is exceptionally useful for linking ideas together in a succinct and logical way. It's worth taking the time to teach children how to use such words properly. Learning to use them effectively is also a great way to make children think deeply about how sentences are formed.

The idea that follows the word 'despite' always has to be turned into a noun phrase or a gerund in order for the sentence to make grammatical sense. This in itself requires children to write something that sounds reasonably sophisticated. For example:

Despite my misgivings, I decided to lend him the money.
I arrived home after her, despite leaving first.

There are also a few other words and phrases that children can use to rearrange their ideas into more succinct sentences:

Unless
Although
Even though
Given that
While
Whenever
Wherever
However
Assuming that
Supposing that
As long as
Even if

Next time you're tempted to ask your pupils to use 'discombobulated' or 'mellifluous' in a sentence, consider giving them one of these instead. You're likely to be making them think a lot harder and, in the end, that will do a lot more for the quality of their writing.

Summary

There are infinite ways in which to arrange the words in any sentence, but only a few of them will make sense. There are some useful words and phrases that you can teach your pupils to help them to link their ideas in a way that will be accessible for the reader. However, the simplest tricks that you can teach them when it comes to rearranging their sentences rely on a solid understanding of grammar. If you can use the language of phrases and clauses with your pupils, it will be much easier to give them feedback and make suggestions when it comes to word order within a sentence.

Where next?

So, now that we have looked at word choices and word order, let's think a bit more about sentence length. We all agree that using sentences of different lengths adds pace and variety to a piece of writing. But how long should a sentence be? Do short sentences really speed up the pace or is that just another meaningless strand of a mark scheme? Let's find out.

Resources and modelled texts

Activity A: Word order

Share these sentences with your class and discuss how changing the word order changes the emphasis in each one. Have a look at the following sentences:

1. The teacher poured herself a second cup of coffee because she hadn't slept well the previous night.
2. Because she hadn't slept well the previous night, the teacher poured herself a second cup of coffee.
3. The teacher, who hadn't slept well the previous night, poured herself a second cup of coffee.

How you arrange the sentence changes whether your reader focuses on the action of the teacher pouring the coffee or the reason why she is tired. The first arrangement assumes that some explanation for the poor night's sleep is going to follow, whereas in the third arrangement it is simply an aside.

Give your class the following sentences and ask them to rearrange the word order. Use the discussion questions to explore the impact that this has on the reader.

The animals, who were not fond of the rain, huddled into the barn.
Despite the wet weather, the children wanted to play outside.
Ms Spencer got to work particularly early in preparation for an important meeting.
After mowing the lawn and tidying the flower beds, Geoff sat on the patio and admired his hard work.
Amber, who was not looking where she was going, tripped over the kerb.
Anticipating their owner's arrival, the cats sat on the window ledge expectantly.
The class, who were usually noisy, were sat in silence in the hall.
Despite the treacherous conditions, the team won their match.

Discussion questions

- What impact does changing the word order have? Does it matter?
- What information do you want the reader to focus on?
- Does changing the order affect the reader's interpretation of the sentence?
- Which arrangement do you prefer and why?
- How does the reader's experience change if you add that information as an embedded clause rather than a fronted adverbial?

With enough practice, your pupils will start to feel confident enough to write and reshuffle their own sentences to add variety to their writing. The following extracts could be used to challenge children who feel confident rearranging individual sentences and are ready to tackle whole paragraphs. By working with an entire extract, your pupils will be able to see for themselves the importance of using a variety of sentence structures and word orders.

Modelled writing

Extract 1: Joe's lunch

This short extract is written entirely in simple sentences. Read through it as a class and challenge them to rewrite it, adding in clauses and phrases and changing the word order when necessary. As with a number of the modelled texts and extracts, this example could be used to teach a number of different concepts. In particular, it could be useful for teaching varying sentence length – which you can find out more about in the next chapter.

Joe's lunch

Sighing heavily, Joe picked up the heavy spade. Gardening was hard work. He had been out here all day. He was exhausted. He glanced down at his battered wristwatch. It was time for lunch. Joe sat down and opened up the tinfoil parcel to reveal his favourite sandwiches: cheese and tomato. He opened up his flask of hot coffee. He reached inside his bag and pulled out the chocolate brownie. He assessed the humble meal, excited to start eating. He ate his lunch sat among the flowers, listening to the hum of the wildlife. What a wonderful day.

Extract 2: The school trip

In this extract, all the sentences start with a fronted adverbial. This is a trap that children can sometimes fall into when they first learn a new grammatical concept; they use it on every sentence. Read this together as a class and your pupils will hopefully hear how strange it sounds. Then – you guessed it – ask them to rewrite the extract to add variety to the sentence structure.

The school trip

Following weeks of planning, the day had finally arrived. Excited to get to school, Sara ran down the stairs, her uniform on and her bag packed. Eager to get to school, she helped her brother put on his shoes and hurried him out of the door. As fast as her legs would carry her, she ran all the way down Amhurst Hill. When she arrived, her classmates were queuing outside the school gates, chattering excitedly. Once she'd said goodbye to her mum, she joined her friend Kit in the queue. Clutching her cup of coffee, the teacher emerged from the building and led the children inside. With a squeal of glee, Sara and Kit ran into the classroom; it was going to be fantastic day.

Narrative poetry

Asking your pupils to tell a story as a narrative poem, especially one with a set rhyme scheme, is a great way to make them think about word order. They simply have to find different ways of arranging their lines in order to make them rhyme. As an example, here is a narrative poem telling the story of the Trojan War from *The Iliad*:

We've a story to tell and a tale to
unfold.
A myth and legend, three thousand
years old.
It starts in the city and Kingdom of Troy
With a brave and ambitious but
hot-headed boy.
He was Prince Paris – the son of
Troy's king.
And no one predicted the trouble he'd
bring.
As Paris returned after hunting
one day
He saw Hermes the messenger god
blocking his way.
'I bring you a challenge,' said Hermes,
'from Zeus,
The King of the Gods, who will not be
refused.'
'What is this challenge?' young Paris
demanded.

'You must make a decision,' Hermes
commanded.
Three goddesses suddenly emerged
from thin air.
Hermes said, 'You must choose who
is most fair.
Who is most beautiful? Solve this
dispute.
Decide whom you favour and hand
her this fruit.'
In Paris's hand, a gold apple appeared.
But a goddess's wrath was a thing to
be feared.
Athena was goddess of wisdom
and war,
She promised him victory, wisdom
and more.
Hera was regal – she made mortals
cower.
She would make him an emperor with
unchallenged power.

He cared not for wisdom nor trying to
be mighty,
And so gave the apple to divine
Aphrodite.
For she offered what Paris truly
wanted from life:
The most beautiful woman on Earth
as his wife.
There was just one little problem,
she said,
For the woman in question was
already wed.
The other two goddesses scowled
and withdrew.
They were his enemies now,
Paris knew.
Hermes was satisfied; Paris had
spoken.
But the die had been cast and the
peace had been broken.
Helen of Sparta, the source of the
chaos,
Was unhappily married to King
Menelaus.
When Paris came visiting, Helen was
love-struck.
That was when matters came truly
unstuck.
Helen and Paris ran off back to Troy,
Which Menelaus, enraged, now
vowed to destroy.
His brother, Agamemnon, was the
Greek king of kings,
Of whom the poet still writes and the
singer still sings.
He raised a great army and one
thousand ships,
And ten thousand warriors with
swords at their hips.
Among them went heroes with names
you might know.

When the King of Kings called them
they all had to go.
Achilles was nimble, his legs lithe
and long;
Ajax was brutal, stocky and strong.
Diomedes was fearless; war was
his art.
Crafty Odysseus was scheming and
smart.
The Olympian gods played their part
in these wars.
Athena and Hera backed the Greek
cause.
The apple had made them enraged
and embarrassed,
But Aphrodite backed Troy, Helen and
Paris.
The Greek army was vast, but Troy
was defended.
Upon its thick walls, the great city
depended.
For ten long years, the Greeks gave it
their all.
But whatever they tried, the walls
wouldn't fall.
The Trojans stood staunch, stout and
strong-willed.
Ajax, Achilles and others were killed.
The Greeks were despairing, and
counting the cost
Of a war that seemed hopeless and
soon to be lost.
But crafty Odysseus came up with
a plan.
And that's when the genuine drama
began.
From driftwood, the Greeks built a
huge wooden horse,
Within which they hid a small part of
their force.
The rest of their armies sailed
swiftly away,

Convincing the Trojans they'd called
it a day.
The Trojans assumed that the horse
was a gift,
Too large to be carried, too heavy
to lift.
In the stout city walls was a stout
wooden gate,
And they threw it wide open, thus
sealing their fate.
They rolled the great horse right into
the town,
The soldiers inside it making no sound.
They waited instead until cover of
night,
Then leaped from the horse, gave its
guards quite a fright.
Then secured the gate and let off a
flare,
And so told their comrades that all
was prepared.

The Greek armies returned to the
beach in their masses.
Then entered the city and reduced it
to ashes.
The men were all slaughtered, the
women enslaved.
The buildings were burned and no
one was saved.
Menelaus killed Paris and burned his
remains.
Helen was brought back to Sparta in
chains.
So this tragic tale is now fully spun:
The Greeks are victorious, the Trojans
undone.
The gods are capricious and mortals
are fools.
In those days and always, it's chaos
that rules.

Chapter 7
Long and short:
Varying sentence length

Now pay attention. This is important. The information that we're about to give you is absolutely fundamental if you want to teach your children to write in an engaging, entertaining way. It's not difficult to understand. It's not difficult to do. But it will ensure that the writing your pupils produce fizzes and crackles with life and energy. This is the real deal.

Now, you wouldn't want every paragraph to be written like the one above, especially in a non-fiction text such as this. It would start to read like an emotive American self-help book. However, the relative lengths of the sentences that we write can have a profound effect on the experience of the reader. It's a very subtle and somewhat mysterious phenomenon but there are some concrete observations that we can make about it, and some very specific tips that we can give our pupils to improve their writing.

Why it matters

So, what effect do long sentences have on a piece of writing and what effect do short sentences have? Your first instinct might be to say that long sentences make the pace of the writing slower and short sentences make it faster. Indeed, there have been Key Stage 2 reading test mark schemes that have made exactly that assertion. You can certainly construct paragraphs that will make it appear to be the case:

> **The waves crashed. The boat cast off. Oars splashed into the water. Orders were shouted. Before long, though, the chaos of the harbourfront was behind us and we sailed serenely out into the calm, blue sea.**

That proves it, right? The contrast between the long and short sentences is definitely having a discernible effect on us as readers. The shorter sentences at the beginning of this short paragraph describe short, sharp actions while the longer sentence takes us into a less hurried part of the story. Shorter sentences speed up the action and longer sentences slow it down. Case closed. Well, hang on a moment. Is it the length of the sentences that is determining the pace of the action in this extract or is it just the descriptions themselves? Let's turn things on their head a little:

> **Waves crashed against the harbourfront as the boat cast off, its oars splashing into the water and its captain shouting orders. Then they were off. The harbour was behind them. They sailed out into the sea. It was calm and blue.**

What, you might well ask, is going on here? Once again, the contrast between the long and the short sentences is still having an effect on us as readers but in completely the opposite way! The long sentence at the start now feels packed and frantic. The short sentences at the end suggest that things have slowed down. Looking at this, you may now feel sure that long sentences speed up the pace and short sentences slow it down, when 30 seconds ago you were convinced that the reverse was the case!

The fact is that the sense of speed or slowness is coming from the words themselves. What is happening in both cases is that the *contrast* between the two is being highlighted by varying the lengths of the sentences involved. By grouping together the things that happened quickly (whether it be with long or short sentences) and grouping together the things that happened slowly *in the opposite way* (whichever way that is), the reader's attention is subconsciously drawn towards that difference. How a writer uses this trick is entirely up to them.

Compare and contrast

You can vary sentence lengths to highlight almost any contrast that you want to make more obvious to your reader. For example, you could use long sentences to describe a heroic character and short sentences to describe a villainous one:

> **Holmes walked calmly up to the edge of the rushing waters, cautious and wary but determined to stand up to his old nemesis. He placed the trademark deerstalker cap on his head and held his chin high, ready for whatever was about to happen. Then Moriarty stepped forward. He smiled the coldest of smiles. He met Holmes' gaze. Then he looked away. Holmes was not an easy man to intimidate but there was no doubting the quickening of his pulse or the shortness of his breath. It was an unsettling sensation for Holmes, accustomed as he was to his own ordinarily unflappable disposition. The silence was becoming unbearable so, at long last, he opened his mouth to say something. But Moriarty spoke first. He looked at Holmes again.**
>
> **'Hello, old friend,' he said.**

Equally, you could use short sentences to describe a heroic character and long sentences to describe a villainous one:

> **Lucy stopped. She stood firm, saying nothing. The witch towered over her and stared, her lip curled into a cruel grimace as she sized up her opponent. Lucy wanted to run. But she stayed strong. Disconcerted by the young girl's display of defiance, the witch hesitated momentarily, but then she lifted her wand and let out a blood-curdling scream. Lucy held her ground.**

In this way, you can draw a reader's attention to the contrast between moments of joy and sadness or victory and defeat. You can contrast strength with weakness, good with evil, excitement with boredom or seriousness with frivolity. It doesn't matter which way around your pupils do it, so encourage them to experiment with both and see which they prefer.

How to do it

The basic formula that you can give your pupils here is actually pretty simple:

1. Identify a contrast that you want to highlight in your writing.
2. Decide which side of the contrast is going to be described with longer sentences and which with shorter ones.
3. Get writing.

However, there are some pitfalls here. For a start, some children may find it hard to arrange their ideas into sentences of a particular type. They will need to draw on all the skills and principles that we have covered so far in this book, especially the techniques that we explored in Chapter 5. Secondly, they may need a bit of help with identifying which elements of their stories contain interesting contrasts that need highlighting; some children find it much easier than others to maintain an empathetic awareness of the reader. Finally, as with almost any tip or trick that we can teach young writers, you don't want them to start relying on it in every single paragraph, or else their writing will become repetitive and predictable.

Hills and valleys

A helpful approach can be to encourage your pupils to treat some of their paragraphs as hills or valleys, which either start with short sentences that get longer in the middle and then get shorter again towards the end or the reverse – they start with longer sentences that get shorter in the middle and then get longer again towards the end.

A 'hill' paragraph might look like this:

> **Theseus turned. The Minotaur stood still, but alert. For a painstaking moment, neither of them moved. Theseus raised his sword slightly, more out of instinct than anything else. However, that one almost imperceptible movement jolted the Minotaur into action. The great beast came lunging head-first toward Theseus, aiming to impale him on its vicious horns. Theseus side-stepped just in time and almost lost his balance, but he found his footing and then wheeled around, swinging his sword with all his might. Despite its immense size, the Minotaur was surprisingly quick and, within an instant, it was back where it had started, snarling angrily at Theseus as it prepared for a second charge. It became clear to Theseus that he wasn't going to win this fight with strength or speed; rather, he would have to rely on his wits. This time, as the Minotaur ran, Theseus stayed where he was and, just before those enormous horns would have impaled him, he ducked. He plunged his sword upward, into the Minotaur's heart, and held it there as his opponent writhed and struggled. Then everything went still and the Minotaur's body thudded, lifeless to the floor. Its blank eyes stared up at Theseus. His victory gave him no great sense of triumph. He felt only pity for the poor beast. But it was over. He had won.**

A 'valley' paragraph might look like this:

Risha stood completely still at the edge of the diving board, looking down in terror at the water far below her and trying to ignore the well-intentioned but somewhat unhelpful shouts of encouragement from her friends. She had jumped from the middle board before, and even that had required courage, but she'd never attempted to tackle the top one until now. She knew, on a rational level, that there was nothing to fear but fear itself, but being rational wasn't always easy. She closed her eyes and tried to summon the single moment of determination she needed. She took a deep breath. She took another. Then she jumped. She had done it. She was plummeting through the air. Her stomach churned with indistinguishable feelings of terror and excitement. Then she hit the water feet-first and carried on downward, a surprisingly long way. Within a moment, she was back at the surface, gasping for breath and waving to her friends, who were cheering and whooping. Slightly bewildered and light-headed, she swam to the side of the pool, her heart still pounding, and climbed out onto the side. Adrenaline coursed through her body as she high-fived her friends and took a moment to savour the sense of exhilaration, before making her way back over to the diving boards to have another go.

Like so many skills that we teach our pupils, not just in terms of writing but in every subject, we eventually want them to develop an instinctive sense of how long each sentence should be. In order to get them there, we need to give them some explicit tips. We need to draw children's attention to the different effects that authors generate when they vary the lengths of their sentences, and we need to encourage them to do it too.

Steady as she goes

Just as variable sentence lengths can be used to highlight contrast and bring a piece of writing to life, consistent sentence lengths will make a piece of writing feel steady and measured. If this were maintained all the way through a story, it would probably make it fairly dull for the reader, although good works of fiction do usually need to include a bit of 'down time' between moments of high drama. However, if your aim is simply to be informative, reassuring and matter of fact, then it can be a good idea to maintain medium-sized sentences throughout. A solicitor's letter or a police report, for example, is supposed to sound formal and unfussy. It is important that your pupils learn this style of writing as well. If they produce a piece of non-fiction writing and they're struggling to maintain a formal, factual tone, then perhaps you could start your feedback by suggesting that they try to vary their sentence lengths a little *less*.

Summary

You will hear a lot of highly dubious claims about the effects of varying sentence lengths in writing. Like so many of the concepts and ideas outlined in this book, this is just one strategy that your pupils can use to improve their writing. Varying sentence structures alone will not make for an interesting and engaging piece of writing. The only thing that we can be sure of is that longer sentences look different to shorter sentences and we can use that difference to highlight contrasts. If pupils are encouraged to practise doing this, it will eventually become an instinctive habit.

Where next?

Having addressed sentence structure, it's time to look at an area of writing that has a number of grammatical conventions: writing dialogue. In the next chapter, we explore the value of using reported speech and the barriers that our pupils may face when using it in their own writing.

Resources and modelled texts

Activity A: Arishka's revenge

Share and read the following extract with your class and discuss how it uses a variety of sentence structures to build the mood and tension. Ask them to think about the impact that varying sentence structure has on the mood of each text. You could ask your pupils to use red and blue pencils to colour in the different sentence types to highlight the fact that the mood 'heats up' as the sentences get longer and 'cools down' as they get shorter. Or you may wish to simply use it as a modelled example of the standard of writing that they could produce themselves.

Arishka's revenge

Arishka walked into the playground. After a while, she spotted Maya. Her former best friend was just a few metres away, talking to Skye. Arishka felt an intense rage burning inside her; how could Maya betray her like this? How could she possibly become friends with Skye after everything that poisonous snake had done? The sense of betrayal was raw and suffocating, like a cold hand reaching inside her and pulling at her very heart. But then, she realised, this was exactly what Skye wanted. She was trying to hurt her – she wanted to make her angry. Arishka decided she wouldn't give her the satisfaction. Calming herself, she walked away. She would get her revenge. But not today.

Next, ask your pupils to choose one of the following topics to write about. Remind them that they will need to use longer and longer sentences to build the excitement and then start making them shorter to calm the mood down again.

- A footballer scoring a goal (from the moment at which the player receives the ball to the moment when play resumes in the centre circle).

- A fox chasing a rabbit (from the moment at which they spot one another to the moment when *either* the rabbit reaches safety *or* the fox finishes its dinner!).

- An Olympic athlete taking a dive in the Olympics (start from the moment at which they put their foot on the ladder – you can decide whether the dive is a success or not!).

- A sprint race on sports day (from the moment at which the teacher shouts 'go' until the end of the race).

- A young child opening a birthday present after weeks of waiting (you can decide whether it's the present that they had been hoping for or whether they are disappointed by the gift!).

- Two family members reunited at an airport after years apart (from the moment at which one of them walks through the arrivals gate).

Activity B: The park

This is a similar idea to the activity in Chapter 6 (which would also work well for teaching varying sentence length). Share this extract with your class and explain that all of the sentences are single-clause, simple sentences. Get your pupils to read this text aloud to one another so that they can hear how monotonous and repetitive the writing becomes. They will hopefully notice how the pace of the text slows down and that there is no tension or drama when all the sentences are the same length. Then ask them to rewrite it, adding in clauses and phrases to extend some of the sentences and deciding which to leave shorter. This activity is far more effective once your pupils are confident with punctuating compound and complex sentences, so make time to consolidate this first.

The park: Version A

It was Saturday. Ella and George were getting ready to go to the park. They had carefully packed up their ball, their snacks and their water bottles. They were both very excited. Ella was looking forward to playing football on the field. George was hoping to go on the climbing frame. They called downstairs to their dad. He was watching television. They ran downstairs to talk to him. Dad looked at them both. He explained that they would not be going to the park this afternoon. George and Ella were so disappointed. They began to cry. Ella demanded to know why they could not go. It did not make sense to her. They had been planning this afternoon to the park for ages. Dad pointed out of the window. Ella and George turned to look out. It was raining.

Next, here is the same text rewritten using a variety of sentence structures. You can use this as a compare-and-contrast activity or simply just to model how to extend and vary sentences.

The park: Version B

It was Saturday and Ella and George were getting ready to go to the park. They had carefully packed up their ball, their snacks and their water bottles. They were both very excited; Ella was looking forward to playing football on the field and George was hoping to go on the climbing frame. They called downstairs to their dad, who was watching television. Eagerly, they ran downstairs to talk to him. Dad looked at them both and explained that they would not be going to the park this afternoon. George and Ella were so disappointed that they began to cry. Ella demanded to know why they could not go; it did not make sense to her, as they had been planning this afternoon to the park for ages. Dad pointed out of the window and Ella and George turned to look out. It was raining.

Activity C: The bull

As we explained in the final section of 'How to do it', at times your pupils will need to slow the pace of a text and keep it steady. This is typically when they are writing a non-fiction piece such as a report. For the pupils who need to practise this, give them 'The bull' extract and ask them to write it as if it were being written about for a newspaper article or a non-chronological report. How does the change of audience and purpose change the structure and pace of the text? Encourage them to simplify the sentences and edit them so that they are consistent in length and structure.

The bull

Pablo Ramirez looked at the bull. The bull looked at Pablo Ramirez. Silence. Two lifetimes were contained in one moment. Then the bull charged, its hoofbeats deafening, but louder still was the bloodthirsty cheering of the crowd. Ramirez whipped the piece of red cloth away and deftly stepped aside, dodging and dancing as the bull thundered past. The first charge was over as suddenly as it had begun. Silence returned to the arena.

Chapter 8

The art of conversation:
Direct and reported speech

Take a look at this sentence:

hello said roy hello said ray how are you roy asked im fine ray replied good roy said well anyway id better be going OK said ray bye roy bye

Anyone who has taught children to write is painfully aware of the importance of accurately punctuating dialogue. We have all come across passages like the one above and tried not to wince as we gently suggest to our pupils that they might want to take a little more care over their punctuation. In this chapter, we will recap the conventions of speech punctuation, as the most skilled and experienced teachers can easily forget some of the details, such as where other punctuation marks go relative to the inverted commas.

Why it matters

While it's essential to set out direct speech accurately, it's equally important that your pupils learn when to avoid it. Once they have mastered the conventions, pupils can be tempted to lean very heavily on direct speech to drive the plot of their story forward:

‘Do you have the key?’
‘Yes, here it is.’
‘OK, open the door.’
‘All right, it’s open.’
‘Great, let’s go inside.’
‘Oh, it’s a bit creepy in here.’
‘Shh, listen.’

This is a slow, clumsy and pretty boring way to tell a story. The dialogue isn't making the reader feel that they know the characters any better. It is also acting as a barrier to the sort of description and narrative that could paint a picture in the reader's mind and build genuine suspense. You should encourage your pupils to use direct speech only when the actual words that your characters are saying are important, either because they tell us something about the character or because they are relevant to the plot. To reinforce this point, let's put the speech punctuation back into the passage with which this chapter began:

'Hello,' said Roy.
'Hello,' said Ray.
'How are you?' Roy asked.
'I'm fine,' Ray replied.
'Good,' Roy said. 'Well, anyway, I'd better be going.'
'OK,' said Ray. 'Bye, Roy.'
'Bye.'

It's certainly more comfortable to read than it was before, but you're probably not thinking 'Wow! I'd love to read the rest of that story!' This conversation is simply not interesting to describe in such detail. If this interaction between Ray and Roy is important to the plot of a story that you wish to write, this would be a perfect time to deploy *reported speech*:

Roy and Ray greeted one another briefly, before going their separate ways.

Reported speech enables the author to tell the reader what was discussed in a conversation (to 'report' on it) without going into tedious detail.

Of course, the exact words that a character uses are sometimes quite important. They might help the reader to understand the character's personality or they might have relevance that only becomes apparent later in the story. On the whole, however, your pupils would be well advised to 'report' most of their characters' conversations, rather than setting them out directly.

How to do it

Direct speech

The conventions of direct speech are outlined in more detail on pages 144–46 of *The Grammar Book*, but to summarise:

1. Inverted commas are placed at the beginning and end of the words spoken by characters, and nothing else.

2. There is no agreed universal difference between using single inverted commas or pairs of inverted commas. It's often a good idea to encourage children to use pairs, as it makes them clearly distinguishable from commas on the line above.

3. Unless it's 100 per cent clear who is speaking, you need a clause attributing the speech to a character, e.g. 'Maliyah said…' This clause can go at the beginning, in the middle or at the end of the speech, and will usually be separated from the speech by a comma.

4. Direct speech will always end with a comma, a full stop, an exclamation mark, a question mark or an ellipsis. This punctuation almost always sits within the inverted commas.

5. Start a new line for a new speaker, including the first speaker in a conversation.

Direct speech is an area where people so often tie themselves up in knots. You will meet very learned, literary people who still think (privately and with some anxiety) that there is some magical distinction between single and double inverted commas that, for some reason, no one has ever shared with them. There is not. The rules and conventions that you know are probably all there is to know. The first rule of grammar is that grammar doesn't actually have rules.

Reported speech

You would think that all young writers would warmly embrace reported speech – it is so much quicker and easier than writing out direct speech. Yet, time and again, it seems necessary to remind them that it even exists as a concept. The issue, perhaps, is that it requires pupils to *summarise* a conversation. Summarising anything requires more cognitive effort than we sometimes imagine – distilling the key points, discarding what is unnecessary and then giving succinct expression to what remains. The key is to think about the purpose and function of a conversation that your characters need to have. So, for example, imagine that a pupil had written this:

> **Joan saw a passer-by and said, 'Excuse me, do you know the way to the station?'**
> **'Certainly,' the passer-by replied. 'You go straight on down this road, turn left at the post office and then right at the supermarket.'**
> **'Thank you very much,' Joan said, and off she went.**

As with many of our examples, there is nothing *wrong* with this extract; the spelling is accurate, the punctuation is sound and the grammar is conventional. However, we seem to be including an awful lot of irrelevant information that serves no narrative purpose. Does the reader need to know the way to this fictional station? Is it significant that Joan will need to pass the post office and the supermarket? Does this particular route tell us anything about Joan or another character in the story? It could be that the answer to one of these questions is 'yes', in which case that's fine – we can keep it as it is. However, it is likely that the exact details of this conversation are irrelevant. So what advice do we give to our pupils?

As always, come back to the question of their reader. What are they trying to do for them? Perhaps they're simply trying to move Joan from one location to another in a way that feels natural and believable. Perhaps they want to remind the reader that she is in an unfamiliar place and she doesn't know her way around. Perhaps they want to show the fact that Joan is displaying initiative. Whatever their aim, they can probably do it without recounting the entire conversation. For example, they could simply write:

> **Joan asked for directions from a passer-by and then made her way to the railway station.**

Reported speech should be a time-saver but it doesn't always come instinctively to our pupils. There is also a problem here that stems from the points that we explored in Chapter 3. Our pupils are used to having to *do more writing*, to *get more lines down* or to *finish the page*. As long as we incentivise this way of thinking, we incentivise mindless waffle… and there is no form of waffle more mindless than pointless direct speech!

Accents, tones and voices in speech

If your pupils want to indicate that a particular character has a particular accent or an unusual voice, they might be tempted to spell that character's direct speech phonetically. Authors do this all the time, and it can be a very effective way to convey the sound of their accent or to create humour. However, we would urge caution here. Children in Key Stages 2 and 3, however bright, have limited life experience, and their understanding of all the subtleties and sensitivities around accents is likely to be limited. At best, their phonetic spellings of words will not be as clear as they think they are. At worst, they run the risk of veering into territory that could be seen as insensitive or even downright offensive toward a particular group. Unless they're exceptionally perceptive and sensitive, children in Key Stages 2 and 3 are better off, where possible, describing the sound of a person's voice themselves and then spelling their words conventionally. To help them to do this, it's worth highlighting and discussing the sort of vocabulary that will enable them to describe accents, tones and styles of voice. Some examples are: *clipped*, *drawling*, *lilting*, *cadenced*, *plummy*, *liquid*, *gentle*, *shrill*, *gravelly*, *acerbic*, *sarcastic*, *haughty*.

Verbs instead of 'said'

In Chapter 5, we explored the importance of selecting precise verbs. This principle is entirely applicable to writing speech and, for very good reasons, English teachers up and down the land will encourage their children to think about the many verbs that they can use instead of 'said'. This is, on the whole, to be encouraged, but it's also important not to go over the top. For example, we have known of teachers who have told children *never* to use the word 'said'. This is a bit silly – it would be like banning the words 'were' or 'went'. If you open any work of fiction on a page containing dialogue, you'll see plenty of instances of the word 'said'. It's a very useful word, and sometimes the dialogue is so important that you want your reader to focus entirely on what is being said, without worrying about whether it is being exclaimed, muttered, hollered or promulgated. It's also possible to give your reader an idea of how words are being said through the other information that you give them about your characters and their actions:

> **Siobhan sat down heavily and sighed. 'So that's it then?' she said. 'We've lost?'**
> **Arisha shrugged. 'We could appeal, I suppose.'**
> **Siobhan raised an eyebrow. 'An appeal? Is that possible?'**
> **Arisha looked wary. 'It's possible… I don't know how successful it would be but…'**
> **But Siobhan was sitting bolt upright now, the fire back in her eyes. 'If there's a chance, then we've got to take it.'**

Notice that the verb 'said' appears only once here, but rather than using lots of near-synonyms or alternative verbs, the dialogue has simply been bolted onto other information about the characters. This enables us to picture very clearly how each line of dialogue would be said. The key here is variety. Direct speech can so easily become monotonous, and your pupils need to keep changing things up if they want it to stay lively and fresh. Your job is to teach them all of these techniques and encourage them to play around with all of them.

Summary

The conventions for setting out direct speech are simpler than people often think. If there are rules that you think you don't understand, you're probably imagining them. One problem when we teach our pupils how to set out speech correctly is that they are likely to overuse this technique.

You should encourage them to use reported speech wherever possible, and when direct speech is called for, to set it out with as much variation as possible, to keep it lively for the reader.

Where next?

Having considered how to teach children to include speech in their writing, we're now moving onto the importance of teaching them to write differently to the way in which they speak. The next chapter is all about different voices and styles.

Resources and modelled texts

Activity A

Share the following extracts with your pupils and ask them to reduce the conversation to one sentence. Here is an example:

Direct speech:

'I think we should go to the cinema this evening,' Freya said.

'I'd prefer to go ice-skating,' Erin replied.

'But you wanted to go and see that film,' Freya pointed out, 'and it's only out for another week.'

Erin thought about this for a moment and then said, 'Yes, that's true. And I suppose we can go ice-skating any time. OK. Let's go to the cinema.'

Reported speech:

Erin and Freya decided to go to the cinema.

Extract 1

'Would you like a cup of tea?' Phillip asked Aman.

'I don't really like tea. Do you have any coffee?' Aman replied.

'Certainly!' Phillip leaped up and marched purposefully over to the kettle. 'Milk? Sugar?'

'Both, please.'

'Coffee with milk and sugar coming up.'

Extract 2

Amie looked at her watch and sighed; she was going to be very late.

'It's delayed,' said the gentleman sitting on the bench opposite.

'I thought as much. How long have you been waiting?'

'About 15 minutes.'

Extract 3

The teacher approached the child, who was hiding behind her parents' legs.

'Hello! Welcome to Reception – what is your name?'

'Anna,' replied the child.

'Hello, Anna! My name is Miss Prothero – would you like to come and play?'

'Yes please.'

Extract 4

'Can I take your order?' the waitress asked.

'Yes please, I'd like a Diet Coke and the club sandwich, with extra cheese and chips on the side,' Sam replied.

'Any sauces with that?'

''Ketchup and mayonnaise, please.'

'Coming right up.'

Extract 5

'I think we're lost,' Emily worried.

'Well, let's look at the map again – pass me your phone, mine is out of signal,' Edgar replied.

Emily handed Edgar the phone; he opened up the map and zoomed into their location.

'Can you work out where we are?' Emily asked anxiously.

'Hmm. I think so – let's go this way.'

Extract 6

'Imogen, can you clear away your toys, please?' Mum called up the stairs.

'But I'm still playing with them,' Imogen replied.

'Well, come downstairs and play with them then.'

'I will in a bit. I'm just doing something up here.'

'Five minutes, Imogen.'

'OK, Mum.'

Modelled writing

There are a number of ways in which you could use these modelled texts. You might want to start by asking your pupils to highlight the examples of direct and reported speech. Then, challenge them to rewrite the direct speech as reported speech.

Fiction

English lessons

It was a grey, Tuesday morning and Ellie was fed up. Her teacher was at the front of the room, droning on about something incredibly dull. Ellie had stopped listening some time ago. It wasn't that she didn't like Ms Edwards; it was more that she didn't like English. Words didn't make sense to Ellie the way that numbers did. Numbers were reliable; they did what you expected them to do. Words were harder to understand and meanings seemed to change all the time. Ellie looked out of the window. It was 9.30 am but was only just getting light.

'Ellie, are you listening?' Ms Edwards' kind voice interrupted Ellie's thoughts.

'Sorry, Ms Edwards, I don't think I understand what we're doing.'

Ms Edwards patiently explained that in today's lessons they were writing the opening paragraph of the adventure stories they had been planning.

Ellie flicked through her book and found her plan. She hated it. Her story was so boring and she couldn't think of a way to make it any better. Why did they have to write adventure stories anyway? What a pointless activity.

Ellie looked at the rest of her classmates busily scribbling away. Ms Edwards was sat at the front with Andrew, explaining to him how to use commas. On the table next to her, Amelie and Amelia were bickering about who had come up with a better ending for their story. Amelie explained that hers was better because it was a cliffhanger, but Amelia said she thought that cliffhangers were for people who couldn't think of a proper ending.

Ellie hadn't thought of an ending for her story. She raised her hand.

'Ms Edwards, I can't think of how to end my story – can you help me?'

'Well, today we're just writing the opening paragraph, Ellie, so why don't you focus on that for now and we can think about the ending in another lesson.'

Ellie sighed. How was she supposed to write a story without knowing how it was going to end? It just didn't make sense.

Suddenly, there was a knock at the door. Ms Spencer, the headteacher, asked for a quiet word with Ms Edwards.

'OK, Year 5 – just carry on with your writing. I am just going to step outside for a minute.'

They left and shut the door behind them. Ellie could see them speaking in hushed tones.

With Ms Edwards out of the room, spontaneous conversations burst out across the classroom.

Adam was telling Dylan about the film he saw at the cinema last night, Annabel was explaining to Ines how to set out direct speech in her story and Cleo was loudly telling her table about the new trainers she got for her birthday.

Ellie rolled her eyes. How was she supposed to work with all this noise?

At that moment, Ms Edwards re-entered the room.

'OK, Year 5 – quieten down please.'

Silence swept across the room. Ms Edwards asked Ellie to read her opening paragraph to her. Ellie sighed and took her book up to the front of the classroom.

Non-fiction: Newspaper report

Wolf vs. Ham: Verdict due today

The world is sitting with bated breath as we await the verdict of the Wolf vs. Ham trial later today. Mr Wolf is suing the Ham brothers for defamation after they claimed that he tried to destroy their homes. Mr Wolf told the jury that he had no intention of destroying the Hams' home, and his huffing and puffing was simply a result of the high pollen count. 'I have hayfever – have done since I was a cub,' he explained.

The pigs, however, told the jury that they believe Mr Wolf had been plotting this act for a long time and it is simply the latest in a long line of terrible things that he has done over the years. Mr A. Ham explained that their vendetta between the Wolf and Ham families goes back decades. He pleaded with the jury to find Mr Wolf guilty as only then would his family feel safe. 'You must understand that if he walks free today, it is only a matter of time before he strikes again. We are not guilty of defaming Mr Wolf's reputation – he did that on his own.'

Away from the courtroom, this trial has split the nation. Polling shows that 52 per cent of people are on the side of Mr Wolf, whereas 48 per cent side with the Ham family. We took to the streets of Hull to find out what people were saying. Dora, 82, told us that she thinks the Ham family should be found guilty and that Mr Wolf has been the victim of a relentless smear campaign by the Ham family.

'I see what they're doing – we all see it,' Dora told our reporter.

On the other side, Timothy, 38, explained to us that he believes that the Ham family deserve justice.

'I see a hardworking family being terrorised by an evil, manipulative wolf. Mr Wolf is suing for defamation because he has been backed into a corner – I can't imagine he will be successful in this case.'

Meanwhile, the 48 per cent have been crowdfunding to raise money to rebuild the Hams' three homes. The fund has raised over £468,000. The creator of the campaign, Mr Good, explained that he knew as soon as he heard what had happened that he had to do something to help.

'I believe that most people are good people and will sympathise with the Ham family during this difficult time.'

The verdict from the case is due at 3.00 pm.

Play script

Use this script and ask your pupils to write it out as prose. The challenge will be deciding which lines should be direct speech and which should be reported.

The spitfire pilot

PILOT:	Fighter Command, Fighter Command. This is Angel One. 616 Squadron. Do you read me? Over.
CONTROLLER:	Angel One. This is Fighter Command. We read you loud and clear, Bertie. Over.
PILOT:	We've hit a spot of bother, Polly. We sighted Gerry over Folkestone. Seven, maybe eight Messerschmitts came out of nowhere. I'm afraid two of our boys bought it. Over.
CONTROLLER:	Where are the German fighters now? We're getting nothing on radar. Over.
PILOT:	They're just coming around for another pass. In fact, they…
CONTROLLER:	Angel One, do you read me? Bertie, this is Fighter Command. Do you copy? Over.
CONTROLLER:	Angel One, I repeat, this is Fighter Command. Do you read me?
PILOT:	Sorry to keep you, Polly. This is Angel One. Over.
CONTROLLER:	It's a relief to hear you, Bertie. Are you all right?
PILOT:	Gerry came back round and we took a bit of a battering. We've taken most of them down but at least two of them are still out there. I…
CONTROLLER:	Angel One? Angel One, do you read me? Over.
PILOT:	Fighter Command, this is Angel One. We got them. Over.
CONTROLLER:	That's good news. Are you damaged? Over.
PILOT:	I'm afraid so. Just me left. The rest of the squadron got theirs. I rather fear my fuel tank has taken a peppering. I'm losing altitude fast. Over.
CONTROLLER:	Can you find somewhere to come down safely? Over.
PILOT:	I think the game's up actually, Polly. Listen Polly, there's something I need to tell you – something I've meant to tell you for a long time. You see, Polly, I lo…
CONTROLLER:	Angel One? Bertie, do you read me? Over.
CONTROLLER:	Angel One, do you copy? Bertie, can you hear me?
CONTROLLER:	Bertie?

Chapter 9
Would that it were so simple: Different voices and styles

In the 2016 Cohen Brothers film *Hail, Caesar!*, Ralph Fiennes plays a stuffy 1950s film director working on a highbrow comedy of errors with an actor (played by Alden Ehrenreich) who is used to portraying action heroes in Westerns and has been hopelessly miscast. One of the actor's lines is 'Would that it were so simple', already an archaic and pretentious deployment of the subjunctive even in the '50s (if you're baffled by it, as well you might be, it essentially means 'if only it were so simple'). An increasingly frustrated Fiennes repeats the line over and over again with ever-increasing fervour, but Ehrenreich's Western star is unable to get his mouth around the words. The scene is funny on several levels and it tells us a lot about society, snobbery and the English language.

George Bernard Shaw famously said in *Pygmalian* (1913) that 'it is impossible for an Englishman to open his mouth without making some other Englishman hate or despise him'. Hopefully, that's not entirely true, but most of us understand the point that he was making. Whether your spoken English could be described as cockney, Scouse, RP (received pronunciation) or rural West Country, life in the UK comes with the less-than-reassuring guarantee that someone, somewhere, is going to be annoyed by the way you talk.

Why it matters

Formality, dialect, register and tone are all thorny and contested issues. We firmly believe that the best way through thorny and contested issues at school is to teach the facts and give children all the tools that they need to navigate the matter themselves. So, that does mean learning to speak and write using formal standard English *in formal situations*. It also means being respectful and mindful of our pupils' backgrounds and the differences that there will inevitably be between the ways in which they use language colloquially. It's a subtle but important distinction. Teaching children to use standard English in writing lessons is an essential part of a teacher's job. Attempting to 'correct' the informal language that children use in their own conversations is likely to come from a place of snobbery and ignorance. Using standard English is a useful academic skill, but it is no better, no more intelligent and no more cultured as a means of communication than any other form of language.

Tone, style, voice, register. There are a number of different terms that we use, overlapping in their definitions, to describe the way in which our words *come across*. When you're writing the fourth email to your broadband provider about an unresolved problem with your internet connection, you will knowingly adopt a decidedly different register to the one that you probably used in the first email. When you're sending a message to a colleague whom you like, know and trust, the tone will be more relaxed than it would be if you were sending the same message to a colleague with whom you have a more tense relationship. These matters are not trivial – they lie at the very centre of the decision-making process in which we engage when we write anything. They're incredibly complex issues, rooted in nuanced norms about the way in which we communicate with one another and the various ways that we interpret subtle social cues. This can make it particularly tricky for some neurodivergent pupils. As a result, we need to give them something solid that they can hold onto: a few concrete principles that will enable them at least to begin finding their way.

How to do it

Formality and informality

Even within the parameters of what we would call 'standard English', register and tone can vary wildly. It is perfectly possible to write relatively informally and still use standard English. The concept of formality is a very hard one to pin down. It's a concept that we learn to recognise through experience, but it is not easy to explain it to children without enough of the necessary experiences. We often fall back on clichés like 'Imagine that you're having tea with the King'. However, that's not necessarily an easy thing to imagine if you've never left Ilford.

As with anything like this, the only way that we're going to adequately communicate the concept of formal language is with plenty of examples. We need to flag up formal writing when we encounter it with our pupils, and we need to point out the features that make it formal. So what are those features? Here, teachers can often fall into the trap that we discussed at the start of Chapter 2. They will talk about the 'macro' features of the text (what it's about, who it's for, etc.) and then dive straight into the 'micro' features (the vocabulary being used). A single word is neither formal nor informal. A sense of formality is largely created in our middle world – at the level of the sentence. Compare and contrast these two sentences:

> **Dave and Eric were yelling at each other, and then had a massive punch-up.**
> **The alleged altercation between Mr Monroe and Mr Collins reportedly followed a heated verbal exchange.**

Now, it probably is valid to observe that the vocabulary in the second version is more 'sophisticated' than the vocabulary in the first. It also seems obvious to us, as adults, that these two sentences would serve different purposes. The first might be an account given to a friend of what had happened. The second might be the language used in a news report or a statement given in court by a lawyer. However, there are some other important distinctions to note, and these are useful distinctions to teach your pupils:

- Formal writing is less personal, whereas informal writing tends to be more personal. In the example above, first names have been used in the more informal sentence. These have been replaced with surnames in the second instance, not as a mark of respect (it is far from clear whether the author of the formal sentence has any respect for them at all) but as a way to make it less personal and less intimate. For the same reason, formal writing is much more likely to use the passive voice, which we will look at in the next section.

- Formal writing seeks objectivity whereas informal writing tends towards subjectivity. The first account above uses subjective descriptions of events – exactly what constitutes 'yelling' or a 'punch-up' might vary from person to person and lead to controversy. They are quite emotive terms. A word like 'altercation', on the other hand, covers a very broad range of possibilities and suggests greater objectivity, signalling the author's emotional detachment from what has happened.

- Formal writing is more likely to use qualifying adjectives and adverbs (such as *reportedly* or *alleged*) so that it appears more measured and circumspect. It is also more likely to deploy slightly euphemistic descriptions (e.g. 'a heated verbal exchange') so as not to sound unnecessarily dramatic.

By flagging up some of these differences, rather than focusing entirely on 'sophisticated vocabulary' or the purpose of the text, you can make the distinction between formal and informal writing a little clearer to your pupils.

Active and passive

Switching between the active and passive voices is a useful way in which to control the level of formality in a piece of writing, and it has a variety of other uses that we will explore in a moment.

The prime minister delivered the speech.

This is a very ordinary simple sentence. It contains a subject (*The prime minister*), a verb (*delivered*) and an object (*the speech*). This, like most simple sentences, is written in the active voice. It introduces the subject and then, through the verb and predicate, it tells us what the subject did, was or experienced. However, what if we don't want the sentence to be primarily about the prime minister? What if we want to emphasise the speech itself? In that instance, we can use the passive voice:

The speech was delivered by the prime minister.

The speech is now the subject of the sentence, we have extended the main verb into a verb phrase (*was delivered*) and the predicate is completed with a prepositional phrase (*by the prime minister*). To express an idea using the passive voice, you will always need to combine the main verb with a version of the verb 'to be':

The food <u>is being provided</u> by a local catering company.
Patients <u>will be seen</u> as soon as the doctor is ready.

Using the passive voice *depersonalises* whatever is being written. As well as contributing to the level of formality, it also changes the emphasis of the sentence, which can sometimes be useful:

A new school has been officially opened by the mayor.

No offence to the mayor, but the star of the sentence above is the new school, and using the passive voice gives it a greater status within the sentence. In the same way, news reports will often use the passive voice to focus their audience's attention on the victim of a crime:

An 82-year-old man has been assaulted by his neighbour outside his home in West Yorkshire.

This sentence makes the 82-year-old man its subject and makes him, rather than the violent neighbour, the focus of our attention and, probably, our sympathy.

Registers

When we write, we can write in any number of *registers*. A piece of writing can be sarcastic, earnest, playful, funny, sentimental, romantic or aggressive. It would be impractical to write a comprehensive 'how-to' guide about how to generate each of these registers – it's all too subtle and subjective. However, it is worth asking your pupils to experiment with different ways in which they can word a particular sentence, and to consider what the various different versions do to the register of their language. For example:

I trust that you realise how impressive that is to me – you are truly incredible.
I suppose you think I'm impressed by that – you are utterly incredible.

Look at these sentences. Their meanings should be almost identical. Almost everything in the second one is synonymous with everything in the first one. Yet the second one is written in an angry and sarcastic register, while the first one sounds far more sincere and, depending on the context, maybe even a little flirtatious! The result is that they have totally different meanings. The differences are so subtle that it's hard to pin them down. 'Truly' and 'utterly' might seem like two interchangeable synonyms for the word 'very', but in the sentences above they create dramatically different effects. In fact, no two words are completely synonymous. It's why it's so important that children learn to rephrase and reword their sentences, to experiment and play around with them until they've got them just right.

Writing as other people

'Writing in role' is a staple of primary English lessons, sometimes to the point that it is relied on a bit too heavily. Those who advocate regular 'writing in role' activities will point out that it encourages children to empathise with a particular character. That is not an invalid point. However, *all* writing should encourage children to empathise with someone else, as their purpose at all times is to connect with their reader. You might want to consider whether it would be worth replacing some 'writing in role' activities with activities in which you write *to* a character in a particular story.

Taking on another person's 'voice' is incredibly hard. Have you ever read a child's attempt to forge a note from their mum because they haven't done their homework? Most children haven't developed their *own* distinctive voice in their writing yet and, as we discussed in the previous chapter, attempts by children to take on another person's tone and inflections can be somewhat problematic. We are absolutely not saying that they shouldn't write in role in their English lessons – it's only by practising that we learn to do anything. However, it probably is a skill on which you don't want to get hung up. If you are asking your pupils to write in role, it would probably be best if you use the activity as a vehicle for the delivery of more specific and more explicit teaching points that will enable them to make immediate progress in their writing.

Moods

It's worth taking a moment here to talk about moods. We don't mean whether a piece of writing is happy or sad; we'll cover that in the next chapter. We mean grammatical moods: indicative, interrogative, imperative, conditional and subjunctive. These are different styles of writing that we use for different purposes, and they are generally formed by using particular verb tenses. The **indicative mood** is the one that we use most often, and it is the grammatical style that we use to make statements:

The president lives in the White House.

The **interrogative mood** is the grammatical style that we use when asking questions. We all recognise it and we all acknowledge that it contains its own conventions, e.g. we usually begin a question with a verb, which is a very unusual thing to do in other contexts:

Can you feel the love tonight?

The only other situation in which it is common to put a verb at the start of the sentence is when we are giving orders or instructions. This is called the **imperative mood**:

Go and sit over there.

The **conditional mood** is the style that we use when expressing what we might do in hypothetical situations:

If I won the lottery, I would buy a yacht.

It's worth noting that we also use the conditional mood when writing stories in the past tense. If we are describing our characters' thoughts and feelings about events that lie in their own future, we use the conditional. Children often find this confusing, and it is a very important point to communicate to them:

Jamal wasn't sure what he would do next.

The **subjunctive mood** (*would that it were so simple*) is used to describe desired or requested outcomes:

I urge that His Majesty make haste.

You can read more about all five moods on pages 153–56 of *The Grammar Book*.

Summary

Register and tone are subtle and fairly mysterious features in writing. However, there are some specific skills that we can teach our pupils to help them to control these aspects of their own writing. We can teach them to make language choices that determine whether their writing sounds personal and emotional or objective and measured. We can teach them to use active and passive voices to shift the emphasis of their sentences. All of these skills will help them to develop their own palette of writing styles, which they can use to produce different types of text.

Where next?

Register and tone are arguably under-taught in primary schools, whereas our next chapter is an area that is taught to death. It's time to address literary devices.

Resources and modelled texts

Modelled writing: Formal vs. informal

Use these extracts to demonstrate the differences between formal and informal writing. You could show your class both texts at once or just show them the formal text and ask them to write the informal version, or vice versa. Use the discussion questions at the end of the text to help you.

The restaurant

Anna has just celebrated her 30th birthday. She had booked to have dinner with her friend in a fancy restaurant but the night did not go to plan. The food and service were both awful. The next day, she writes an email to her friend Katie to tell her about the evening; she also writes an email complaining to the manager of the restaurant, demanding compensation for the awful evening.

Formal letter of complaint

Dear Sir/Madam,

I am writing to you following a disappointing experience at your restaurant, on Friday 5 August. I had booked a table for eight to celebrate my 30th birthday. Upon arrival at the restaurant, the staff seemed to have no knowledge of our booking. Rather than apologise and arrange a table, the member of staff simply shrugged and explained that we would have to wait. If I had known how the rest of the evening was going to go, I would have left at that point. However, it was my birthday and I did not want to spoil the mood so we ordered a drink at the bar and waited for 40 minutes for a table to become available.

Once we were seated, the waitress came over to explain that several of the items on the menu were no longer available, including the dish that I had been planning to order: the seafood risotto. While I appreciate that it can be difficult to predict how busy a restaurant is going to be, as a top restaurant in Central London you should have learned to plan for this. At this point, it feels appropriate to mention the waitress, who was rude and impatient. At one point she rolled her eyes while we were choosing our meals and abruptly dismissed any additional requests such as my sister's request to have extra dressing with her salad. She also forgot the water for the table and had to be reminded three times, which, given that it was 38 degrees yesterday, made for an uncomfortable wait.

And my goodness did we wait. It took over 40 minutes to receive our starters and by the time they arrived one of the dishes was cold and had to be sent back. The wait for the main course was not much better and I have to say that I was disappointed with the quality of the food by the time it arrived. The steak I ordered was overcooked and rubbery; the vegetables were limp and certainly past their best; the chips were cold. I raised this with the waitress at the time, who explained that we could send the meals back but there would be a long wait until we received a replacement dish. By this point I was ravenous, so I ate the sub-standard food but requested that the meal be removed from the bill. The waitress acted as though this was a ridiculous request and explained that if I was choosing to eat the meal, I would have to pay for it.

Following the ordeal with the main courses, we decide to forgo desserts and instead ordered a round of teas and coffees. It seems that even this was too much of a challenge for your staff. They sent oat milk instead of soy milk, cappuccinos instead of lattes and took the order for fresh mint tea but then claimed they were out of mint. The bill arrived with my main course still itemised, despite my request to have it removed. I queried this with the waitress, who said that she was not able to authorise a reduction at that time.

I am incredibly disappointed that what was meant to be an evening of celebrating ended up being an evening of disappointment and frustration. The service was slow, the staff were rude and the food was inedible. I have enclosed a copy of our receipt and am requesting a full refund to compensate for the miserable evening that we had. Needless to say, I will be not returning to your restaurant any time soon, so would not accept any sort of complimentary meal as compensation.

I look forward to your response.

Yours sincerely,
Ms A. G. Grieved

Email to Katie

Hi Katie,

Don't worry about not being able to make the meal last night – I wish I had missed it, to be honest! Do you remember how excited I was to go to this restaurant? Well, it was a nightmare from start to finish. They lost our booking so we had to wait 40 minutes for a table, and the waitress had a real attitude problem and barely cracked a smile all evening. She was miserable and rude; at one point she even rolled her eyes at us – can you believe it? Even once we eventually got to our table, things continued to go wrong. Half the food on the menu was no longer available for some reason, they forgot our water and, when my main course finally arrived, it was disgusting. I mean seriously disgusting. The steak was rubbery and gross; I didn't even know you could cook steak that badly. The vegetables weren't much better – they looked like the sort of thing you might find lurking at the back of the fridge – rank. Even the chips were cold and soggy – what sort of restaurant can't even get chips right? And this place wasn't cheap, you know?

Obviously, I kicked off but the waitress was having none of it. She wouldn't even take my meal off the bill! How mad is that? What happened to the customer is always right? Anyway, today I'm writing to the manager to get my money back, so hopefully they'll listen.

Anyway, looking forward to catching up soon. Lunch would be great – I don't mind where we go – although I know where we WON'T be going!

Love,
Anna xx

Discussion questions:

- Read the two texts – in what ways are they different? Are there any ways in which they are the same?
- Which text is more formal? Why?
- What is it about this text that makes it more formal?
- What do you notice about the greetings/sign-off of each email?
- Why is the tone of the two emails so different?

Hotel review

You can have a lot of fun discussing the register and tone of this hotel review:

Review of the Hotel Paradiso in Manaus

Mr Clement Atkinson-Featherstonehaugh
0 stars

My wife and I have stayed at many different hotels all over the world. We fully appreciate that, due to cultural differences and the way in which people's expectations vary from one country to another, one must be open-minded when making a judgement about a particular establishment. However, even taking that into account, I am afraid to say that our stay at the Hotel Paradiso was thoroughly miserable from the moment of our arrival right through to that blessed time when we were finally able to check out.

To say that the staff were discourteous upon our arrival would be a considerable understatement. The unsmiling gentleman sitting at reception did not even look up from the newspaper he was reading when we arrived; he merely handed us a key and grunted. No one was on hand to assist us with our bags and, other than being woken in the middle of the night by a very loud argument between two of the younger members of staff, we barely saw another hotel employee for the entire duration of our stay.

The rooms themselves were small, dirty and foul-smelling. The carpets were encrusted with various unidentifiable stains, the curtains were torn and the beds were crawling with lice. The wallpaper was peeling off, several items of furniture were cracked or chipped and neither of the bedside lamps would turn on. The walls were paper-thin and, as a consequence, one was all too aware at all hours of the conversations going on outside one's own room, including the aforementioned altercation between the chambermaids. For this same reason, we were reluctant to discuss anything of a personal nature, even in the privacy of our own room, for fear of being overheard.

The communal bathrooms were too few and their condition, if anything, was inferior even to that of the bedroom. Our floor, where at least 60 guests were lodged, was served by two cramped cubicles, into each of which a bath tub and a lavatory had been inelegantly installed beneath the leaky ceilings. On one occasion, it appeared from the sights and smells that greeted me as I entered that someone had been unclear as to which of these two facilities was which. The conditions of the bathrooms perhaps exemplified better than anywhere else in the hotel the general attitude of indifference and disregard shown towards cleanliness and hygiene.

The Hotel Paradiso is the cheapest hotel in Manaus and yet still manages to be awful value for money. Should I ever visit Manaus again, I should be happy to pay twice as much to stay somewhere that I would deem fit for human habitation. I would not recommend this hotel to my worst enemy. It is unsuitable accommodation for anyone, even a farm animal. 'Paradiso' is Portuguese for Heaven. If this is what Heaven is like then, when I die, I should be happy to take my chances in Hell.

Chapter 10
Literary devices

You may have been surprised not to see more in this book so far about literary devices – metaphors, similes, alliteration, etc. We have nothing against these tools and it's certainly a good idea to teach children about them. However, there is a tendency to flog them to death in this country and also to teach them in a strange, disembodied way. The message that we give children is that using these tools is somehow a good thing in and of itself, without giving any real thought to the purpose of the devices or their effect on the reader.

There also seem to be some pretty arbitrary conventions about which literary devices we spend time teaching. Many children know what personification means by the time they leave primary school. Few know what anaphora means. Yet it's by no means clear that the former is more important, more straightforward, more common or more useful than the latter. It's quite possible that *you* don't know what anaphora means, dear reader. Fear not – you're not alone, and all will be explained in this chapter.

Why it matters

Let's begin our discussion of literary devices by looking at the old favourite: similes and metaphors. The first interesting thing to note about similes and metaphors is that the meaning of these words has shifted over time and our profession is probably responsible. Originally, a simile was a literal comparison to something that was, in fact, comparable. For example:

At eight weeks old, a foetus is about the size of a kidney bean.

There is no poetic licence being used in this sentence – a foetus at eight weeks old is, quite literally, about the size of a kidney bean. Originally, a metaphor was a figurative, exaggerated or non-literal comparison of any sort. For example:

My love for you burns like the sun.

That is a cheesy, corny example, but then similes and metaphors are usually quite cheesy and corny. The interesting thing about the original distinction between metaphors and similes is that it was actually quite a useful and important distinction. It can be important to know whether a comparison is being made to provide literal clarification or to make a point using poetic imagery.

Of course, you're reading this section and thinking that the distinction you've learned (and taught) between a simile and a metaphor is something subtly different. We all accept the modern teacher's orthodoxy: that a simile is when you use the word 'as' or 'like', whereas a metaphor is when you just say that the thing you're describing *is* something else. So, we would identify 'My love for you burns like the Sun' as a simile and only recognise it as a metaphor in a form like this:

My love for you is a burning sun.

The equally interesting thing about *this* distinction is that it is utterly *un*interesting and gives pupils absolutely no extra information about when to use a simile and when to use a metaphor. We've reached the point where we can't escape these definitions of a simile and a metaphor – they're so ingrained that children will drop marks on tests if they don't accept them. However, it probably is worth discussing the original distinction with them too, as it is a far more interesting one when selecting the right descriptive language for a particular task.

All of this brings us back to the main point that we always want to keep in our minds when teaching children to write: what effect will their writing have on the reader? Will a simile or a metaphor make their description better? More vivid? Easier to picture? Great, then use it. Will it slow them down and muddle their picture of what is being described? If so, leave it out. This goes for all literary devices. Before we dive in, we want to urge caution about teaching these to your pupils as 'good things to include' in their writing. They are tools. Like all tools, pupils should use them when they're useful and leave them in the box when they're not.

So, we're going to look at several different literary devices (we'll take similes and metaphors as read) and explore what they are, what they do and when they're useful.

How to do it

Personification

OK, we're not going to take similes and metaphors as read completely. It's worth taking a moment to look at a particular type of metaphor (in both senses of the term) that is particularly useful. Personification, as you'll be aware, means talking about non-human objects as though they are human:

The clouds wandered lazily across the sky.
The camera loves you.
Mondays don't agree with me.

We like personification. Why? Done well, it's simple, it's succinct and it builds a picture in the reader's mind very easily. Human beings are primed to see design and intention in everything. Furthermore, we will knowingly and unknowingly ascribe human-style consciousness where it doesn't occur (think of utterances like 'my new phone is refusing to connect to the internet' or 'the gears are very stubborn'). In philosophy, this is called anthropomorphism, and it is very useful to us as writers. We can describe movements or feelings in a very relatable way by comparing them to the movements or feelings of people.

Just one note of caution – it is possible to overdo personification:

The trees were waving their wooden arms in the breeze, twitching their leafy fingers.

This might as well just say, 'Look at me, I'm using personification in my writing.' They most certainly are using personification; they just aren't adding anything useful to their description by doing so.

Pathetic fallacy

Pathetic fallacy is essentially a form of personification in which the setting of a story or the objects within it are described as though they have emotions befitting the events of the story itself. The term 'pathetic fallacy' is a confusing one because both words are being used in an archaic way. 'Pathetic', in this sense, is the adjective form of the noun *pathos*, an emotional connection with the story, which we will explore in the next chapter. A fallacy is something that is misleading and false (used, presumably, because settings, objects and weather don't really have feelings at all). The obvious example of pathetic fallacy is when weather is described as being gloomy or menacing in order to create a spooky atmosphere. Equally, if you describe a mild, sunny day with a gentle breeze, you will create a relaxed, calm atmosphere, which might set the scene for a relaxed, calm scene or, conversely, might serve to misdirect the reader before something terrible happens!

Look at the first three lines of 'The Highwayman' by Alfred Noyes, that staple of Year 5 and 6 English lessons throughout the country, which begins with a generous (dare we say it, possibly slightly excessive) helping of pathetic fallacy.

The atmosphere of 'The Highwayman' is sinister and deadly but romantic and mysterious, so the wind, the moon and the road are described as if they are all those things. Pathetic fallacy is a very useful tool for your pupils to use if they want to create a particular atmosphere for their reader.

Onomatopoeia

The spelling bee favourite, onomatopoeia means using words to describe sounds that sound a bit like the sound that they describe:

Crash, bang, wallop.

The main thing to tell our pupils about onomatopoeia is not to use it too often. Particularly when attempting to narrate action or fight scenes, some children can fall back on onomatopoeia as an alternative to actually explaining what the hell is going on:

Whoosh! Bang! Now there were two secret agents in the plane firing. Pow! Zap! Crash! Another plane flew in. Rooooooooar. Now they were fighting. Smash.

A child writing something like this is obviously imagining something very exciting. We just don't really know what. Rather than describing it fully, they've merely told us what noise it makes. As always, good writing comes back down to empathy with the reader. Onomatopoeia is rarely doing the job that children think it is. If you come across a piece of writing like this, go back to Chapter 5 and then have a chat with the child about using precise verbs and nouns!

Anaphora

If you don't know what anaphora means, you're probably worried that it's something very complicated. Allow us to reassure you:

> **This little piggy went to market**
> **This little piggy stayed at home**
> **This little piggy had roast beef**
> **This little piggy had none**
> **This little piggy went wee wee wee wee all the way home.**

Anaphora means using the same words and phrases repeatedly to bring cohesion or to emphasise a point. It's incredibly common in poetry, nursery rhymes and songs. You'll find it everywhere, from the hymn 'All things Bright and Beautiful' to 'Every Breath you Take' by The Police.

You may be thinking, 'Can't we just call that "repetition"?' And the answer is: Yes. You can.

Triplication

By the same token, if you don't know what triplication is, you're probably worried that it, too, is something very complicated. Allow us to reassure you once again!

> **We will stand. We will fight. We will prevail.**

Stuff sounds cool when you say or write it in a similar way three times. That's what triplication is – a specific type of anaphora in which the repetition occurs precisely three times. It's not clear why three is the magic number but it is. Saying or writing something in a similar way three times in a row almost always sounds cooler than saying or writing it twice in a row or four times in a row.

If your pupils want something to sound inspiring, defiant, emphatic or determined, encourage them to use a bit of triplication. It's simple, it's easy and it's effective!

Other literary devices

There are hundreds if not thousands of other literary devices that have been identified and written about over the years, from well-known concepts like alliteration (beginning a succession of words with the same sound) to more obscure concepts like anthimeria (using one word class as another) or the wonderfully named synecdoche (when a part of something is used to describe the whole, such as asking for someone's *hand* in marriage). Some everyday words to which children need no introduction, like *sarcasm* and *humour,* started out life in the classical world as terms for literary devices. We could go through dozens of these concepts individually, exploring the purpose of each one. Ultimately, however, the question that you and your pupils should be asking yourselves never changes: how does this affect my reader?

Persuasive writing

In Chapter 1, we urged caution about teaching persuasive writing as a list of 'features'. However, there is a time and a place for a bit of tub-thumping rhetoric, and there is no harm in encouraging children to try out a few literary devices in that context. It can be productive and quite fun to get them writing inspiring, motivational speeches in the mould of *Braveheart*. Admittedly, you might have an issue with the age rating of *Braveheart*, especially as the speech itself contains the slightly post-watershed phrase 'bolts of lightning from his arse'. However, you can usually link inspirational speeches to other historical figures that your pupils might be studying: Churchill, Elizabeth I and Martin Luther King are probably the three most obvious examples. A bit of anaphora and triplication goes a long way in their speeches!

Summary

The curriculum can be a little arbitrary and unpredictable when it comes to the technical terms for the literary devices with which it expects children to be familiar. When it comes to the actual quality of their writing, learning these terms is interesting but not crucial. What matters is that pupils have the opportunity to observe and notice the different techniques writers use, and to consider what purpose they serve.

Where next?

Some of the literary devices outlined in this chapter are used to elicit an emotional response from the reader, whether that's anger, pity or fear. In the next chapter, we will look at other strategies for creating this emotional response.

Resources and modelled texts

Modelled writing

Trapped

Have a look at these two texts; one of them includes every literary device under the sun. Read through it with your class and ask children to identify as many as they can. Then discuss with your class the experience of reading this text – it's jarring and difficult to understand. The next extract is the same piece of text but with barely any description or literary devices. As a class, compare the two extracts and then challenge your pupils to write a text that strikes the right balance between the two.

Blearily, Adam opened his eyes and tried to get a sense of where he was. He was in a cave – a freezing cold cave. Icicles stared down at him, shining like diamonds; frost hugged the ground, biting at his fingers. Adam stretched out his legs and pushed himself up onto his feet. As cautiously as a tightrope-walker, he stepped out onto the ground in front of him. CRACK! Adam leaped back – the ground wasn't concrete. It was ice – very thin ice. His heart sunk like a rock falling to the bottom of the sea. There was no way out; no way home; no way back to his family. All hope was lost and despair pulled him into a suffocating embrace. Adam put his head in his hands and sobbed; his tears were a river running down his face. He howled like a wolf to the moon but there was no one there to hear him. After what felt like an eternity, he slumped down in the corner, exhausted. He had no tears left, his heart shattered like the ice on the lake and his throat was hoarse. He closed his eyes and drifted off into a world of sleep.

 CRACK! SPLASH!

Adam's eyes snapped open. Something must have stepped on the ice and fallen through. He cautiously approached the hole in the ice, like a lion tamer approaching a lion. He gasped, his icy breath cutting his throat. It wasn't something. It was someone.

Blearily, Adam opened his eyes and tried to get a sense of where he was. He was in a cave – a freezing cold cave with icicles and frost. Adam stretched out his legs and pushed himself up onto his feet; he stepped out onto the ground in front of him. CRACK! Adam leaped back – the ground wasn't concrete. It was ice – very thin ice. His heart sunk; there was no way out. All hope was lost. Adam put his head in his hands and sobbed. After what felt like an eternity, he slumped down in the corner, exhausted. He had no tears left. He closed his eyes and drifted off to sleep.

A loud crack snapped Adam out of his slumber. Something must have stepped on the ice and fallen through. He cautiously approached the hole and gasped. It wasn't something. It was someone.

Shackleton's speech

This is an imagined speech written as a stimulus for a Year 5 class who had been learning about Shackleton's journey to Antarctica. You might want to encourage your pupils to read it aloud, thinking about intonation and pauses, before discussing the features of this speech and attempting to write their own.

Ship and stores are gone.
It's bitterly cold and constantly dark.
And we're stranded hundreds of miles from anyone who could rescue us.

I'm not going to lie, men, we're in a tight spot and no mistake. And I know what you're thinking. I know what you're thinking because I've thought it too, late at night when my darkest fears haunt my mind – oh yes, I've thought it.

You're thinking that we don't have a chance.

Stuck out here on the ice floes of Antarctica without our ship! What odds do we have of ever getting home? What hope do we have of survival? No one has ever survived anything like this. That's what any normal man would think.

But, my friends… we are not normal men.

Normal men don't sign up for expeditions like this – they don't have the stomach for it.

Normal men wouldn't even get this far – they wouldn't have the courage or the resilience.

Normal men would have given up already.

Five thousand men applied to come with us on this expedition. Five thousand. Most of *them* were normal. And I didn't choose them.

I chose you.

I chose you because I knew the dangers we faced. I chose you because I knew that when the going got tough, you'd have what it took to survive. I chose you because, my friends, you are brilliant and you are brave.

It's going to be tough, it's going to be painful and, heaven knows, it's going to be cold. But when your family see you again on that dockside in Plymouth when we return, when you tell your parents about your adventures or hold your children in your arms again, you'll tell them of the challenges you faced and you won't regret one minute of it.

Because you won't be you anymore. You'll be someone changed. You'll be wiser, stronger and braver than that man who left England six months ago. We set out to cross Antarctica from one side to the other. Now our mission is survival… but I tell you, the fame and glory you signed up for is still yours to claim. When we survive this, every newspaper in Britain will plaster its front pages with tales of your accomplishments. In a hundred years, school children will still learn about your deeds. Most people die and are eventually forgotten but your names will live on. Frank Worsley, the unsinkable captain, Frank Hurley, the fearless photographer… even you, Percy Blackborrow, the stowaway – perhaps I won't eat you after all!

I swear to you, my friends, my *brothers*, it all still lies before us. The greatness and the glory we set out to claim will still be ours. Stand up, dust yourselves down and prepare yourselves for the fight of your lives. We are the crew of the *Endurance* and we will not be defeated.

We are going to succeed, we are going to survive and, by God, we are going to claim our place in history. Now let's get to work.

Chapter 11

Make me feel: Eliciting an emotional response from the reader

We humans like to congratulate ourselves on being such rational creatures, capable as we are of evaluating the past, assessing the present and planning for the future. Yet, deep down, we all know that it's our feelings that really drive us. Our hopes, our fears, our likes and our dislikes generally lie at the heart of our real motivations for most of our actions. Politicians know this and use it to their advantage. The most rational and logical arguments can find themselves trounced at the ballot box by ideas and even slogans that chime with voters' feelings. So, if you want your writing to have any impact on your reader at all, you have to reach them on an emotional level. This is a complex and inevitably sensitive matter, but it's a fascinating one too, and absolutely crucial if you want your pupils to become competent writers.

Why it matters

We believe in teaching children about the features of the English language rigorously, using proper technical terms. Typically, our fiercest opponents will argue that such an approach stifles children's creativity and prevents them from expressing themselves. There are two major problems with this argument.

The first is that it is plainly not true. A child with a competent grasp of English grammar is likely to have a greater range of tools at their disposal when deciding how to express their thoughts and feelings than a child who has only a limited vocabulary with which to discuss language. If you want a child to compose music, a good first step is to teach them how musical notation works. If you want a child to paint, you'll save them a lot of time if you show them that you can make green by mixing blue and yellow. Why would the technical processes behind creative writing work any differently?

The second problem with arguing against the teaching of grammar as a defence of self-expression is that it completely fails to understand what writing is for. It is there to be *read*. It is not enough that we teach children to express their thoughts and feelings into an unheeding void. We want them to be able to communicate their thoughts and feelings to others. The genius of Beethoven is not that he was able to feel things any more or less acutely than anyone else; it is that he was able to *make us feel them too*, and he was able to do so in a unique and beautiful way. If we are sufficiently ambitious for our pupils, then we must teach them to do exactly that when they write.

Obviously, all art forms elicit different responses from different people. An opera that moves one theatre-goer to tears might leave another entirely nonplussed. A film that terrifies one viewer might seem laughably corny to another. Those who consume art bring their own experiences and associations to it, and these will dramatically colour their responses. We are all different; none of us can get inside anyone else's head and there are no totally safe bets when we are looking for ways to influence other people's feelings. If we get it wrong, we run the risk of ending up like Monica from *Friends* in the eighth-season episode 'The One in Massapequa'. Ross and Monica's parents are celebrating their 35th wedding anniversary and Monica is very excited to be delivering a speech at the celebration, as this responsibility has usually fallen to her brother Ross. Ross has a reputation for delivering very moving speeches, which reduce the audience to tears. Monica makes it her mission to outdo Ross in terms of the emotional response that she elicits from the audience. The result is an embarrassing and over-the-top performance that makes no one cry, but which does make us, as viewers, cringe.

The line between Beethoven and Monica Gellar can be a subtler one than you might think. However, once children can write with a degree of conviction and control, there are some general principles that we can teach them to make it easier for them to land emotional punches.

How to do it

Suspense

Let's start where most teachers quite rightly start. Perhaps the easiest (if far from easy) feeling of all to elicit in a reader is suspense. It's the easiest because it's fairly obvious how it works. Building suspense requires three ingredients:

1. introducing an intriguing mystery or unanswered question to your reader
2. waiting a while before revealing the solution to the mystery or the answer to the question
3. regularly reassuring and reminding your reader that the solution or answer is coming.

Anyone, even a less confident writer, is capable of following these three steps. Not only is suspense a fairly simple feeling to elicit, but it's also a very useful one for the writer as it keeps your reader engaged. The challenge for your pupils is to think of a sufficiently intriguing mystery or unanswered question to begin with. You will need to give this careful thought during the planning stage of children's writing (see the next chapter).

Pathos

Generating pathos – genuine pity from the reader on behalf of one of your characters – is hard. It requires the reader to truly suspend their disbelief and immerse themselves in the story as though it were real. In the first instance, this generally means that all of the story's other features need to be rock solid. If a piece of writing is riddled with grammatical or spelling errors, if the wording of the sentences is unclear or clumsy, or if the narrative is flat and boring, the reader is not going to invest their emotion in it. Even if all those elements are there, creating pathos is a challenge, but it's not a complete mystery. There are some tools that we can give our pupils.

For a start, alluding to tragedy or loss is often more effective than stating the facts straight away. Consider this famous extract from *A Christmas Carol* by Charles Dickens:

> **'Spirit' said Scrooge, with an interest he had never felt before, 'tell me if Tiny Tim will live.' 'I see a vacant seat,' replied the Ghost, 'in the poor chimney-corner, and a crutch without an owner, carefully preserved. If these shadows remain unaltered by the Future, the child will die.'**

The Ghost need only utter the final four words of his response to answer Scrooge's question. The rest of it is gathering pathos – ominously building to the horrible truth by describing the tangible realities of Tiny Tim's absence. The image of the empty chair at the dinner table is something of a cliché, although it might have been more novel when Dickens used it, yet it perfectly encapsulates the way in which pathos is generated by writers. By describing the physical effects of the character's absence, we make the reader do the rest of the mental work. They will build the rest of the picture themselves, including the feelings of the characters who are left to mourn. The image of the crutch, carefully preserved, makes us imagine Tiny Tim's family in the aftermath of their loss – unable to fully accept the pain of their loss by disposing of the crutch that is no longer needed. Crucially, however, none of that is spelled out. We, as readers, are left to do just enough heavy lifting ourselves. As we do so, we draw subconsciously on our own real experiences of grief and loss. This is, no doubt, a big part of why we can enjoy sad books and films. They enable us to express and process, at a safe distance, some of the complex feelings and emotions that dwell within us. This phenomenon is known as *catharsis*.

However, all of this highlights a limitation when we're teaching these skills to young writers. They have far less of their own experience to draw on. If they're lucky, some of your pupils may not yet have experienced real grief or loss. If that is the case, they're more likely to have success at creating pathos if they start small – perhaps by describing the death of a hamster, rather than a human child!

There is another interesting observation to make about the extract from *A Christmas Carol*, and it is the line about Scrooge himself. The fact that he has become so concerned with Tiny Tim's wellbeing (indeed, he asks about his fate 'with an interest he had never felt before') means that we, Dickens' readers, are suddenly filled with hope and optimism. This is one of the first signs of change in Scrooge – that the heartless old miser from the beginning of the story is starting to change his ways. Dickens skilfully creates a moment of hope and optimism that makes the gut-punch of the Ghost's response all the more brutal. Darkness is darker and light is lighter when each is contrasted with the other. A skilled writer switches between the two, quickly and deliberately. Nothing is more effective as a means to toy with your reader's emotions!

Imagine that you were watching a war film and, in a quiet moment, one of the characters spoke the following line to one of their comrades:

> You know, when this war is over, I'm finally going to propose to Stella. We'll get our own plot of land, just like we've always talked about. We'll get a cow, a couple of pigs and some chickens. We'll plant some apple trees and we'll start a family.

One thing is certain, right? That character is going to get killed in the very next scene! Hope and despair rely on one another. Contrast is key.

Happiness

Contrast is also essential if your aim is to make the reader feel happy and optimistic. A happy ending to any story comes after a struggle and the threat of an unhappy ending. In *A Christmas Carol*, the darkness and misery of the first four staves is what makes the fifth and final stave so joyous – the contrast between Scrooge as he was and as he has now become. One of the last things that Dickens tells us is that Tiny Tim did not die – again, all the more uplifting because we were made to think that he would.

However, it's not just about the ending. Throughout a story, main characters need moments of peril (literally or metaphorically) and moments of deliverance – where the peril is lifted from the character's shoulders. The more convincing the moments of peril, the more joyful the moments of deliverance. The key is to keep taking the reader on a roller coaster. This seems obvious to us as adult readers, but to our pupils it might not be obvious unless we point it out.

Melancholy

Melancholy is not quite the same as sadness. It is, perhaps, a very specific type of sadness. When you look through a photo album from your childhood, you might experience a touch of melancholy – not a cold, hopeless sadness, but a feeling of wistful, thoughtful nostalgia. It can actually be quite a warm and even strangely pleasant feeling. It is the emotion that makes us well up during a moving speech at a wedding and it is the mood that often makes Year 6 leavers' assemblies such poignant occasions. It is a mysterious and actually rather beautiful instrument in the orchestra of human emotion, enabling us simultaneously to mourn and celebrate the passing of time.

How do you explain it to an 11-year-old, let alone teach them to elicit it in someone else through their writing? Obviously it's not easy, but a good way in is through stories containing flashbacks. You may have come across the short animation 'The Piano' by Aidan Gibbons, a charming short film (only two and half minutes long) in which an old man sits playing a piano as he is 'visited' by his memories. Children only half-understand the fact that old people genuinely used to be young people, and stories with flashbacks are a great way to make them really see it. They are also a good way to discuss sentimentality, nostalgia and poignancy.

Flashbacks in films and on TV often depict the memories of people who are old in the present day. An interesting way to turn this on its head is to ask your pupils to write stories set in the future, when they themselves are old, and set the flashback in the present. There's an example of a short story that does this on page 112. For children, this makes it slightly easier for them to imagine that the older person's memories really are their own.

Inspiration and motivation

So far, we've looked entirely at the feelings that can be stirred in readers of fiction. What about non-fiction? Very often, we want readers of non-fiction to come away inspired and motivated by what they've read. Part of that, of course, has to be achieved simply through the content. If the information contained within a non-fiction text is sufficiently interesting or the arguments are sufficiently convincing, then the reader is likely to come away enriched by the experience.

However, style and language choices do come into it too. An appallingly written book about an interesting topic is still an appallingly written book. By the same token, excellent writing can bring less scintillating subject matter to life. A task that is always worth the time with Key Stage 2 and 3 pupils is speech-writing. It gives them the opportunity to play with some of the literary devices that we looked at in the previous chapter (triplication, anaphora, etc.) and to test the effect of their language choices on an audience.

Summary

Human emotions are complicated and often mysterious phenomena. However, good writing has to reach its reader on an emotional level. This is never an exact science but there are techniques that we can teach our pupils to build suspense, pathos and joy. We can help them to build melancholy and poignancy into their writing and we can give them tools that will help them to inspire and motivate an audience.

Where next?

This brings us to the end of Part Two. In this section, we have spent a lot of time looking at word choices, sentence structures and strategies for making your reader feel. The next section is all about that painful process of actually getting your words down on the paper. And it starts with planning.

Resources and modelled texts

Suspense

Ask your pupils to read this paragraph and describe their feelings as they do so. Discuss the techniques that have been used to build suspense throughout the paragraph.

> Creeeaaaak… the floorboards cried as Jacob took a tentative step towards the oak chest. The attic was a place of secrets, covered in cobwebs. A place of shadows and whispers. A solitary light bulb hung from a low, wooden beam and flickered as if it

was about to come to the end of its days. In the corner, an old battered armchair sat gloomily, lost of its original purpose. No one had entered the attic for years and John noticed that the once pristine wallpaper was now torn and peeling. The carpet was threadbare and a cloud of dust was hanging over everything, clinging for dear life. As he opened the chest to retrieve the old pair of wellington boots that he was planning to bring on his trip to the Lake District, something glinted in the corner of his eye. He slowly turned in the direction of the shiny metal surface – out of place in this dimly lit ramshackle room. It was face down on an old bedside table stripped of its drawers, and would be seemingly innocuous to anyone else except Jacob. He knew exactly what it was…

Single-sentence suspense

In 1948, Fredric Brown published 'Knock', a short story that consisted of just two sentences. It's the world's shortest horror story and it goes like this:

> **The last man on Earth sat alone in a room. There was a knock on the door…**

Share this with your pupils and discuss why it is so chilling: the reader fills in the back story and comes up with their own bleak theory about what has happened to everyone else on Earth. Challenge your pupils to write their own single-sentence suspense story. Once they have that idea, they could then work that single sentence into a short story of 100 words, then 500 words, etc.

Modelled writing

Flashback

This story is designed to help pupils to empathise with an older character. Initially, it is set in the distant future and your pupils will probably find it easiest to identify with Serena, a girl visiting her grandfather. Once the flashback kicks in, the grandfather's memories take him back to his childhood, during the Covid-19 pandemic. If you're reading this book within a few years of its publication, then you will be teaching children who will suddenly realise that it is the grandfather who is their own age, not the granddaughter. When the story returns to the future, this might help them to tap into the wistful sense of melancholy that a flashback can create.

The capsule glided noiselessly to a stop outside Grandpa's house. Serena climbed out and walked up the driveway. The sensor above the door scanned her retina and the front door slid open. Grandpa was sitting in a large armchair, watching a music video on the hologramophone.

'Hi Grandpa,' Serena said, 'who's that?' She pointed to the young woman singing in the video.

Grandpa smiled. 'You won't have heard of her. Her name was Taylor Swift. She was one of the biggest pop stars in the world when I was your age.' He muted the video. 'And how are you today, Serena?'

Serena sighed, 'Yeah, fine.'

'Ah,' Grandpa said knowingly, 'that sort of fine. The sort of "fine" that isn't really very fine at all.' Serena said nothing, so Grandpa pressed on. 'Care to tell your old grandpa what's bothering you?'

'Just… everything,' Serena said. 'I started a new school in September and I've found it hard to make friends. The work is really hard, my teachers are all really strict and it's been a real challenge. I've tried to be resilient, I really have. I thought I'd made a new friend and I thought I was getting better at maths but then today I fell out with my friend, I got a rubbish score in my maths test and I just…' Despite her best efforts to control herself, Serena started to cry. 'It just never seems to get any better. I feel like I'm just going round in circles.'

'Oh, I know that feeling,' Grandpa said, standing up unsteadily and coming to sit beside Serena.

'You do?'

'Of course. Life is full of these challenges – difficult situations that seem to go on forever. Just when you think things are about to get better, something goes wrong and it feels like you're back at square one.'

'You've had that feeling too?'

Grandpa laughed. 'More times than I can count. I found myself constantly out of work in the mid-2060s, in the economic chaos during the second wave of the Climate Crisis – that was like going round in circles. My first marriage was a bit like that too.'

'Your first marriage? You mean…?'

'Your grandmother was my second wife. Did your mother never tell you that? Oh, believe me Serena, I know what it's like to feel trapped in a hopeless situation.' He looked up at the silent image of the old-fashioned pop star on the hologramophone and something – the shadow of a memory perhaps – flickered across his eyes. 'In fact, I was in a situation a bit like that when I was your age. The whole world was.'

'Really?'

'Oh yes,' Grandpa said. 'Have you ever heard of Covid?' And then, seeing her blank expression, he added, 'The coronavirus?'

Serena frowned. 'I've had viruses. I had a cold last week.'

Grandpa shook his head. 'Not *a* virus,' he said. 'At the time, people called this *the* virus.'

'What happened?' Serena asked.

Grandpa took Serena's hand. She looked at the contrast between his old, wrinkled, papery skin and her own: smooth and youthful. Grandpa's skin must have looked much the same once upon a time, she thought, and one day hers would look as thin and ancient as his did now. 'It's so long ago now,' Grandpa said, his eyes fixed on some distant, invisible point, 'but I remember it like it was yesterday.'

'February at the earliest?!' James's dad was shouting at the television. Well, to be precise, he was shouting at the prime minister. James's heart sank. The original lockdown had been exciting at first. A dramatic global crisis had forced all the schools to close – most children would have thought they'd be celebrating! But, as the months wore on, there had been less and less to celebrate. Online learning was better than nothing and it offered James a connection to his friends and teachers... but it could never replace actually being in school.

When schools reopened to all their pupils in September, James had been overjoyed to see his friends again. It felt like life was getting back to normal. He'd believed the pandemic might even be coming to an end. Now it was like the whole awful business was starting all over again: a 'new variant' was what the people on the news kept saying. On and on it went – on and on and round and round.

'They say the worst of it should be over in a couple of months,' James's mum said reassuringly.

'They always says that,' his dad retorted. James had been thinking the same thing.

He trudged upstairs to the little room that Mum called the study and turned on the laptop. Teams hadn't been reactivated yet and there was nothing from his teachers on the school website. He picked up the football he'd been given for Christmas just the previous week and threw it up in the air disconsolately. It was brand new – white, shiny and immaculately clean. He caught it and threw it again but this time he lost control and it landed with a crash in a tray full of stationery.

'Stop playing with that thing inside!' his dad shouted up the stairs. 'That's not what it's for.'

'No,' James muttered to himself, 'it's for playing football with my friends. And I won't be able to do that for weeks – maybe months.' He couldn't even go and play outside on his own because it was pitch black. He hadn't been able to see his grandparents or his cousins over Christmas. He hadn't been able to go and see his friends either. He didn't even know when he'd next be able to go on holiday.

It just feels like we're going round in circles, he thought miserably. *This is never going to end*. He opened his email inbox. His friend had sent him a link to a Taylor Swift video. *And I hate Taylor Swift,* James thought to himself.

Serena looked sceptically at her grandpa. 'Is that story supposed to make me feel better? That was thoroughly depressing!'

Grandpa slowly rose from his chair, his knees creaking. He walked slowly over to a large chest in the corner of the room and opened the lid. From the chest, he produced an old, battered, mud-stained football.

'I've kept it all these years,' he said, handing it to Serena.

'Why?' she asked, reluctantly accepting the filthy looking thing.

'Look at it,' he said. 'It's worn, dirty and tatty.'

'Er, I can see that,' Serena replied.

'It's worn, dirty and tatty,' her grandpa repeated, 'because it was *used*. The pandemic didn't go on forever – *nothing* in this world goes on forever. The world returned to normal and the schools reopened – *permanently* this time. Everyone saw their friends and relatives again. They hugged and played and had parties. They travelled, they went to concerts and I played countless football matches with my friends with this very ball. It all came back and, in 72 years, it's never gone away again. I've kept the ball all these years to remind myself of that moment, back in January 2021, when everything felt so bleak. I've kept it to remind myself that a new day always comes. However dark it gets, the sun will always come out again. And one day, when you're old and frail like me, and *your* grandchildren are having troubles of their own, maybe you'll tell them about the problems you're having at school right now and they will just be a distant memory.'

Serena hugged her grandpa. He wouldn't have been able to hug his grandparents when he was her age, she realised. He wouldn't even have been able to go to school, and yet here she was complaining about having to do exactly that.

'One thing didn't change, though,' Grandpa said.

'What was that?'

'I still hate Taylor Swift.'

Grandpa turned off the video and returned to his seat.

Part Three

Writing it down

Chapter 12
Planning to fail: Planning, drafting, editing and rewriting

You will be familiar with the well-known aphorism 'fail to plan – plan to fail' and there is certainly a significant degree of truth in it. When we dive into any project – not just a piece of writing – without taking the time to anticipate the challenges that we're likely to face, then those challenges will exact a greater cost in time and resources. However, you'll be equally familiar with (at least the first half of) Robert Burns' observation that 'the best laid schemes o' Mice an' Men gang aft agley', which, in less poetic terms, means 'however well you plan something, stuff is going to go wrong'. Since there is clearly some wisdom in both of these apparently contradictory ideas, how are we to plot a course between them?

Perhaps there is an argument for saying that we should plan but we should actually plan to fail, at least the first time around. We should be aware that our pupils' planning, important though it is, will never deliver a perfect finished article on its own. We have to build in the time for them to redraft and to edit. These are essential skills for any writer.

Why it matters

All writers plan. Some plan by making pages of handwritten notes, others by drawing elaborate maps of imaginary lands (Tim), some plan simply by reading and thinking, and others by making notes on their phone on their commute (Zoë). When we think about the process that we went through to plan the book that you're holding in your hands right now, we can identify several stages. Initially, it was just the occasional chat about what our next book might look like. Then, once we hit upon the idea of developing young writers, we spent months doing just that – planning lessons, reading, researching and discussing what was working. By the time we came to pitch the book to Bloomsbury, the book was already planned and the written proposal was a summary of each chapter. It's worth noting too that, like most plans, it keeps changing as we write.

We all agree that planning matters. It's the time when you get your ideas in order and start to flesh them out. The more time and thought that you give to your plan, the easier the writing process will be (in theory). The problem with teaching planning, due to time constraints, is that we often resort to asking our pupils to complete a printed planning form rather than actually getting them to think about what they're going to write. We hand out a story mountain and assume that filling in five boxes is the same as planning a story. Creating a mind map of facts about polar bears might provide our pupils with more knowledge of polar bears but it doesn't actually help them to plan a report – it provides no sense of purpose or information on how they're going to link their ideas. Completing a written lesson plan template (in schools that still have such things) should be the last and least important stage of a teacher's planning; similarly, completing any form of planning template should be the final step for your pupils.

Why have we called this chapter 'Planning to fail'? Isn't that unnecessarily negative? Well, yes and no. Planning is no substitute for the editing that is going to have to happen once you start writing. Here we have to make a crucial distinction between planning and drafting. A first draft sketches the outline of a piece of writing but we always have to go back and colour it in. We plan, we draft and then we *edit*. In fact, if a piece of writing is any good, we probably go round and around those three stages numerous times. A good plan is hardly ever going to enable your pupils to get perfect lines of flowing text down on paper straight away. What a good plan will do is give them a destination for their writing, and there is an important point here that we often don't make clearly enough to our pupils: writing must be planned backwards.

The first thing that your pupils need to decide, if they're writing a story, is how it ends. Consider a murder mystery story – the fundamental piece of information that the writer needs to establish straight away is the identity of the killer, even though this is one of the last things that they will reveal to their reader. The rest of the story, after all, is an exercise in obscuring the truth, misdirecting the reader and yet ensuring that essential clues are left in plain sight. The entire story is a journey to the final outcome. This is not just true of detective fiction – all stories are a journey to a destination. The author needs to know how their characters are going to develop and how the events of the story will unfold. They need to know what twists will occur so that they can set them up. Everything they do over the course of the story is about taking another step towards the final goal. A good story must be planned backwards from the end.

This is equally true of non-fiction writing. The famous part of any Winston Churchill speech is the peroration – the dramatic climax. That's where you find the lines like 'we shall fight them on the beaches' and 'this was their finest hour'. Churchill dictated his speeches to long-suffering Downing Street secretaries, whose unenviable task was to go back and make constant changes as he tried out different wordings and edited the text. However, he always knew roughly where he was going and the key message that he would convey at the end. Everything else in the speech was designed to prepare the listener to receive that message as enthusiastically as possible. In any piece of non-fiction writing, the author needs to know what they are going to be concluding at the end – otherwise the text will be a rambling stream of consciousness.

How to do it

Whether they're writing fiction or non-fiction, it is important that your pupils know which audience they are writing for and the purpose of the text. In an ideal world, it would be a real audience who are actually going to read the text, e.g. 'We're going to write non-chronological reports about polar bears to share with Year 5 at the end of term.' If it's fiction, the purpose could be: 'We're going to write a story around the theme of *lost and found* to engage and entertain Year 3.' This isn't always possible but, at the very least, it's always worth ensuring that your pupils get to read *each other's* writing. If your pupils are writing to no one, they may feel that the task is pointless, and they'll be absolutely right.

Fiction
The structure

When it comes to planning fiction, the story mountain is the go-to structure in primary schools. It divides the story up into five simple parts. Typically, the five parts are:

1. **The introduction:** Here the reader is introduced to the setting, characters, etc.
2. **The build-up:** At this stage, we get to understand the characters a bit better, and as the plot develops, it becomes clear that there is a tension or problem developing.
3. **The dilemma or conflict:** The main problem comes to a head – it could be a battle with an enemy, a personal problem to overcome or a tension within a friendship.
4. **Resolution:** The conflict is resolved (or not!).
5. **Ending:** The reader reflects on the journey that the character has been on, loose ends are tied up, etc.

This structure has at least one seriously prestigious proponent: almost every Shakespeare play is divided into five acts that roughly follow this pattern. Obviously, what we've outlined here is a simplified version of the five-part structure, and most of the novels that you read will break from this to add in twists and turns or endings that set up a sequel. But for children who are learning to write, this is a simple way of structuring their narratives. You'll also spend a lot of time pointing out this structure to them when you read together, or when you've watched a film. Get your pupils to take stories that they've read and break them up into these sections – the more familiar that they are with this structure, the better.

Later on, you might want to introduce them to the 12 stages of the 'Hero's Journey'. This structure was developed by the screenwriter Christopher Vogler based on Joseph Campbell's book *The Hero with a Thousand Faces* (1949). It roughly encapsulates the plot of every adventure story ever written, from *Shrek* to *Star Wars*. Here is an approximate outline of the stages to the Hero's Journey, with some examples from well-known films and books.

The Hero's Journey
Stage 1: Ordinary world
It's called 'ordinary world' but that does not mean that it has to be an ordinary world. It simply means the world in which the character exists at the start of the story. It is where the details of the character's day-to-day life are established.

Examples:

*   In *Shrek*, the ordinary world is Shrek in his swamp.
*   In *The Lord of the Rings*, it is Frodo in the Shire.

- In *Harry Potter and the Philosopher's Stone*, we meet Harry living under the cupboard at 4 Privet Drive.

Stage 2: The call to adventure

At this point, our character's way of life is changed or threatened in some way that calls them into action. It could be something as simple as receiving a letter, or as dramatic as losing a family member, but essentially the call is a catalyst for the rest of the story.

Examples:

- In *Star Wars*, R2-D2 shows Luke Princess Leia's message, asking Obi-Wan Kenobi to help her.
- In *The Lion King*, Scar kills Mufasa and tells Simba to leave the Pride Lands.
- In *Finding Nemo*, Nemo is captured by scuba divers.

Stage 3: Refusing the call to adventure

At this point, the reader or viewer is willing the protagonist to take up the adventure but the character is hesitant or reluctant to go. It could be because they are aware of the risks that they would face or don't feel adequately prepared. In some cases, other characters will try to prevent the protagonist from taking up the call. Often, once the call has been refused, something will happen to raise the stakes and force the protagonist's hand.

Examples:

- In *The Lord of the Rings*, Frodo is reluctant to leave the safety of the Shire.
- In *Home Alone*, when the burglars first attempt to break into Kevin McCallister's home, he turns the lights off and hides under the bed.
- In *Harry Potter and the Philosopher's Stone*, Mr Dursley tries to hide the letters from Hogwarts from Harry.

Stage 4: Meeting the mentor

The mentor is a character who guides and supports the protagonist to take up the call, often equipping them with the skills, strength or resources that they need to take on the adventure. The purpose of the mentor is to build the protagonist's courage and convince them that they are capable of tackling whatever challenges may come their way. Often, they will 'cross the threshold' (see the next section) with our protagonist and help them to navigate their way in the new world. It's a stereotype that the mentor is always an older, wiser character, but this is not always the case. It can often be a character who seems farcical and who the protagonist underestimates to begin with (think Shrek meeting Donkey).

Examples:

- In *The Lion King*, Simba meets Timon and Pumba in the rainforest.

- In *Finding Nemo*, Dory, despite her forgetful nature, ends up mentoring Marlin.
- In *The Lord of the Rings*, Gandalf plays the role of the mentor.

Stage 5: Crossing the threshold

With the mentor's support, our protagonist is now ready to embark on their journey. The threshold refers to the point at which they leave the 'ordinary world' behind and start their adventure in the unfamiliar world. One thing is for sure – there is no going back at this point.

Examples:

- In *The Matrix*, Neo takes the red pill and 'wakes up' from the Matrix.
- In *Beauty and the Beast*, Belle agrees to take her father's place and stay as a prisoner in the Beast's castle.
- In *Shrek*, Shrek and Donkey embark on their quest to rescue Princess Fiona.

Stage 6: Tests, allies and enemies

Having plucked up the courage to embark on the adventure, our protagonist is faced with a number of challenges and obstacles to overcome. With each test, the character learns more about themselves and their abilities; we also learn more about their flaws. It is in this stage that we find out which characters are friends and learn more about the enemy. This is an important stage, as the hero of the story builds up their allies in preparation for the ordeal ahead.

Examples:

- In *The Wizard of Oz*, the Wicked Witch of the West throws a number of tests at Dorothy and her newfound friends, from flying monkeys to sleep-inducing poppies.
- In *Shrek*, Donkey and Shrek face a number of obstacles on their quest to save the Princess, including a fire-breathing dragon (who turns out to be a love interest!).
- In *Pride and Prejudice*, Elizabeth Bennet is tested by Mr Wickham and Mr Collins but gains strength from her father, who is her ally.

Stage 7: Approach to the inmost cave

In this stage, our protagonist learns more about the risks of the challenge that they face. This challenge could be a place that they have to get to, a person they have to defeat or even an inner demon to conquer. One thing is for certain – our hero is facing great peril. They may once again have doubts about whether they should continue their journey, or begin to lose hope, or turn once again to their mentor for support. Before the next stage, the protagonist needs to have gathered up their strength and determination.

Examples:

- In *Harry Potter and the Philosopher's Stone*, Ron, Harry and Hermione plan to get the stone before Snape.

- In *The Matrix*, the Oracle tells Neo that he will have to choose to save himself or save Morpheus.
- In *Jurassic Park*, the approach to the inmost cave is arguably the moment at which the T. rex escapes the paddock. This splits our characters into two separate groups, each of which then have to face their own ordeal.

Stage 8: The ordeal

At this point, the hero faces their greatest challenge so far and their journey appears to be in jeopardy. This could be the death of their mentor or another loved one, a defeat in a major battle or even the end of a romantic relationship – it may look like all hope is lost. But the hero will emerge from the ordeal with newfound knowledge and strength. For overcoming this ordeal, our hero is given a reward.

Examples:

- In *Star Wars*, Obi-Wan Kenobi dies, as Luke and his friends are surrounded by stormtroopers.
- In *The Lion, the Witch and the Wardrobe*, Aslan is murdered and the White Witch raises an army.
- In *Percy Jackson and the Lightning Thief*, Percy Jackson faces Hades.

Stage 9: The reward

Having survived the ordeal, our hero is given a reward. This reward could be a physical item, e.g. a sword to help them with other battles, or it could be newfound knowledge, insight and inner strength. The reward will help the hero to complete their journey. This stage also gives the protagonist (and the reader/viewer) time to celebrate and catch their breath before continuing their journey. This section is sometimes called 'seizing the sword', as the protagonist builds on their progress so far and finds the strength to carry on to the final conflict.

Examples:

- In *Star Wars*, Luke, Princes Leia and Han Solo escape with the plans to the Death Star.
- In *The Lion King*, Simba's father tells him to remember who he is, giving him the strength to go on to challenge Scar.
- In *Spider-Man*, Spider-Man saves Mary Jane and learns the identity of the Green Goblin.

Stage 10: The road back

Boosted by the reward, the hero recommits to the journey and continues with renewed confidence. They continue on with the quest, pursued by an ever-increasing threat. The road back has one final challenge to overcome before our protagonist can return to the 'ordinary world'. During this stage, the stakes are raised to heighten the drama of 'the resurrection'.

Examples:

- In *The Lord of the Rings*, this is the stage where Gollum tries to take the Ring from Frodo at the ledge of the volcano.
- In *Jurassic Park*, our heroes are in the visitor centre, trying to get to the helipad that will take them away from the island.
- In *The Lion King*, Simba returns to Pride Rock and finds that it has been destroyed by Scar and the hyenas.

Stage 11: The resurrection

This is the moment to which our journey has been building: the final life-or-death challenge that our hero must overcome. This could be a final showdown between a hero and villain, the big battle or the moment at which the world is saved. Two things typically happen in this stage:

1. The hero needs to be brought back from the brink of destruction/death (hence the resurrection).
2. The hero is victorious in defeating the enemy.

The battle is not just a battle for the hero's life but for the safety of the ordinary world.

Examples:

- In *The Lion King*, Simba defeats Scar.
- In *Matilda*, Matilda scares Miss Trunchbull into leaving town for good.
- In *The Wizard of Oz*, Dorothy throws water on the Wicked Witch of the West and she melts away.

Stage 12: Return with the elixir

The hero completes the journey home and returns a changed person. Having overcome great peril, our protagonist is stronger and wiser. The elixir refers to the reward that the hero receives, and this could be a physical item such as treasure or, in Shrek's case, the return of his swamp. It could even be new wisdom or knowledge for the hero to share with the ordinary world. Or maybe the real reward was the friends that they made along the way – that sort of thing.

Examples:

- in *The Lion King*, Simba is declared the king of Pride Rock.
- In *Matilda*, Matilda helps Miss Honey to get her house back and Miss Honey adopts Matilda.
- In *Home* Alone, Kevin McCallister's family returns home.

Once you have shared this structure with your class, they will start spotting it in the films that they watch and the books that they read. We have created a child-friendly version of the 'Hero's

Journey' and a planning template that you can use with your pupils – see the modelled texts and resources on page 130.

Generating Ideas

One of the most common problems that children who are confident writers face when they're planning a story is that they are overambitious. They set up a fantastical world and exhaust enormous time and effort describing the characters and setting only to realise that their story needs to be completed in three weeks and they have run out of time – which is why we end up with stories that end like this:

> **Suddenly 'ah!' there was alien! The man had a fight with the alien. The alien had a gun. The man had two guns. Then the alien had three guns. Then there was another man. Then there were more aliens. Then there were more guns and more fights and more men and more aliens. Bang bang bang. Zap. Oh no. Ah. Then suddenly the aliens all died. The end.**

There is a separate discussion to be had about the problem of teaching writing in two-to-three-week units but that's another book in itself. So for now, one of the most helpful tips that you can give your pupils is to plan for the time limit that they have, keep the story simple and get to a resolution. The average sentence is 15 words long and the average word takes 1.2 seconds to write. Even a fairly fast writer will need to spend at least one second thinking for every second that they spend writing. That means that a sentence will take an adult who is writing quickly 36 seconds to write. To write thoughtfully and carefully, most people need at least a minute to craft each sentence – often more. The most important lines in films and plays are edited and re-edited for days. Unless your lesson is several months long, your pupils are not going to be able to write a complex science-fiction or fantasy story in one lesson. Encourage them to stick to a simple idea involving places and characters that they can describe vividly – that usually means writing mostly about their own experience.

For example, if we were writing a story about 'lost and found', then your structure could be as simple as 'a woman loses her dog and finds him again'. The premise might not be overly exciting but, with a simple plot and structure, your pupils' working memory is free to focus on how they tell the story. Another issue that children face when planning their stories is 'thinking of an ending' to the elaborate world that they have set up. The solution to this, as we have already established, is to get them to think of the ending first. What is it that they want the character to have learned by the end of the story?

One Year 6 class that Zoë taught came up with the story of 'Forgetful Bob' and it became shorthand for 'a simple story told well'. We had been trying to write a story about a character learning something about themselves and improving themselves. For this, we needed the character to have a flaw and, after some entertaining discussions about what it could be, we hit on being forgetful. From there, the story wrote itself. Within five minutes we had jotted down the plan on the opposite page.

In the process of coming up with this story, dozens of variations were discussed: maybe Bob doesn't replace the plants and has to face up to the neighbour's anger. Maybe the lesson that he learns is that he shouldn't make promises he can't keep. Maybe the problem wasn't that he forgot to water the plants but that he forgot where he'd put the keys. For those who

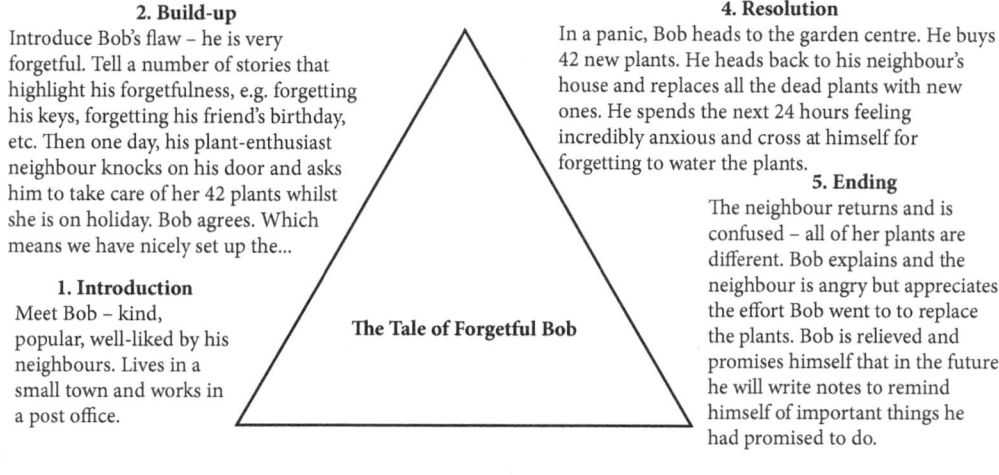

3. Problem
The neighbour leaves for her holiday and Bob forgets to water her plants. He realises 10 days later, the day before the neighbour is due to return. He lets himself into her house, but all of her precious plants have died.

2. Build-up
Introduce Bob's flaw – he is very forgetful. Tell a number of stories that highlight his forgetfulness, e.g. forgetting his keys, forgetting his friend's birthday, etc. Then one day, his plant-enthusiast neighbour knocks on his door and asks him to take care of her 42 plants whilst she is on holiday. Bob agrees. Which means we have nicely set up the...

4. Resolution
In a panic, Bob heads to the garden centre. He buys 42 new plants. He heads back to his neighbour's house and replaces all the dead plants with new ones. He spends the next 24 hours feeling incredibly anxious and cross at himself for forgetting to water the plants.

5. Ending
The neighbour returns and is confused – all of her plants are different. Bob explains and the neighbour is angry but appreciates the effort Bob went to to replace the plants. Bob is relieved and promises himself that in the future he will write notes to remind himself of important things he had promised to do.

1. Introduction
Meet Bob – kind, popular, well-liked by his neighbours. Lives in a small town and works in a post office.

The Tale of Forgetful Bob

wanted an extra challenge, perhaps there could be another twist after the resolution – maybe the neighbour's flight is delayed, so he has to spend another week caring for the new plants.

Working backwards removed the fear of not being able to think of an ending and meant that we could be creative with the rest of the narrative structure. There is a template in the resources section that you might want to use to support your pupils with planning backwards; however, remember that the recording of the plan is the last stage of the planning.

Misdirection

An important consideration when planning a story is *misdirection* of the reader. A genuinely gripping story must contain twists and surprises. To make these compelling, you need to make the reader feel as though the truth was right under their nose the whole time, yet you also need to ensure that they don't spot it too soon. To do this, you need to plan distractions and omissions. Distractions are events in the plot that will keep your reader's attention focused elsewhere. The obvious example of this is creating one or more 'red herring' suspects in a murder mystery. However, some twists require you to omit certain things from the plot. For example, if you plan to reveal that character B is a figment of character A's imagination, then you need to minimise situations in which Characters A and B find themselves in the company of a third person. If you plan to reveal that a seemingly shady character has actually been assisting the hero all along, you need to ensure that none of their seemingly malign actions ever do any real harm. In the resources section of this chapter, there is a very short story called 'Mrs Nethercott', which demonstrates misdirection in a straightforward way.

Non-fiction

There is a temptation to focus on structure when teaching non-fiction texts. The structure is important but, before that, you need to make sure that your pupils know enough about the subject they are writing about to write a report and that they have something to say about it. You may want to link to the history or science that they have been learning so they already have some background knowledge, rather than asking them to research a topic from scratch.

When planning an essay, report or any other non-fiction text, it will help if your pupils know exactly what each paragraph is going to be about. Get them to map out the key point of each paragraph and then, once they have this step sorted, they can start thinking about the order. Once they have a clear idea of these, they can use cohesive devices to link paragraphs and create a sense of fluency (for how to teach this, head to Chapter 14).

Essay-writing

Perhaps the most valuable non-fiction writing skill that we can give our pupils is the ability to write essays. It will help them in exams and, for those who go to university, it is likely to remain a big part of their lives for years to come. Most of us know from experience that those pupils find themselves at a considerable advantage if they reach the sixth form with solid essay-writing skills. So when should we start teaching children how to structure an essay? The fact is that there is no reason not to start at primary school. If you give them a clear structure, they can all have a decent stab at it, and from there they will only get better with practice. We suggest starting out with a simple question about a book that they've read (for example, if they have read *A Monster Calls* (Patrick Ness, 2011), the question could be: 'Is the monster supposed to be kind?') and challenge them to answer it using a three-paragraph structure, before progressing to a five-paragraph structure (or perhaps extending those who are ready with the five-paragraph version):

Three-paragraph structure

1. Paragraph 1: Introduce the question and define the key terms (e.g. what do we mean by kindness?).
2. Paragraph 2: Summarise both sides of the argument, with quotations or evidence.
3. Paragraph 3: Give your own opinion.

Five-paragraph structure

1. Paragraph 1: Introduce the question, define the key terms and give a hint as to your own view.
2. Paragraph 2: Outline one side of the argument, with quotations and evidence.
3. Paragraph 3: Outline the other side of the argument, with quotations and evidence.
4. Paragraph 4: Outline your own opinion, with supporting quotations and evidence.
5. Paragraph 5: Summarise the key points from paragraphs 2, 3 and 4, before ending with a relevant philosophical or meaningful observation.

If you model and support their work at every stage, there is no reason why this should be beyond the vast majority of children in a mainstream Year 6 class.

Editing

Once we've planned to fail, the failing can begin. The very first words that we typed when we started writing this book have almost certainly gone now, washed away by the tides of constant editing and re-editing. The first words that we write can be utter rubbish – they're little more than a springboard to get us started. As with so many things in life, if we keep failing to write something decent, over and over again, we will eventually succeed. This is a difficult message for our pupils, who are likely to see success and failure through the same flawed, binary lens that affects so many adults.

There is another barrier here caused by the disconnect between the way in which we teach children to write and the way in which we, as adults, write. At the time of going to print, most writing in most English lessons in most schools is almost certainly handwritten. Most adults, by contrast, do very little of their writing by hand. Once again, it's interesting to reflect on the way in which we have written this book. It was typed on a Google Document – whenever we finished a chapter, we would read through it and make any necessary changes. We would then read one another's chapters and make further edits. Finally, and most importantly, it then got sent to our lovely editor, who would suggest even more edits. By the time this book was published, 18 months after it was first started, it looked very different to our first draft. If, every time we had wanted to make a change, we had had to go and cross out what we had written and rewrite it by hand, the process would have taken much longer. In fact, we would probably have lost the will to live in the process. We're not suggesting that you chuck out your exercise books but, for longer texts, do consider word-processing to allow your pupils to edit instantly.

However, we need to model editing. Often, when we do this, there is a temptation to focus on correcting spelling and grammar. We have no objection to correcting spelling and grammar, far from it, but you want your pupils to be able to make more sophisticated observations about each other's writing: 'you don't need to spend so long describing his hat', 'this section would make more sense if it came after this one', 'you could have waited longer before you revealed that and created more suspense', etc. Using a visualiser, you can edit a piece of writing as a class very easily. As you do so, through your questioning, you can lead your pupils to some of these more fundamental observations about what needs to be improved. You can use something that you've written yourself or perhaps the work of an anonymous pupil from a previous year. If you're going to use the work of a child in the class that you're actually teaching, we would encourage you to make absolutely sure that they feel comfortable about it. Some children will be delighted to see their writing shared with everyone on the screen or whiteboard; others will be mortified.

Classroom management

If we give children the time that they need to plan, draft and edit their work properly, we quickly encounter an age-old problem: managing the class. Some will work through the stages of the task more quickly than others. As a result, some will be finished sooner than others. This is a book for teachers and we have no desire to teach our proverbial grandmother how to suck eggs (weird idiom that, isn't it? No one is really sure where it came from). However, we also don't want to come across as head-in-the-clouds theoretical types, ignoring the practical day-to-day realities of working in a school. So it is worth acknowledging that you do need to plan your lessons carefully if you are going to give your pupils meaningful time to plan, draft and edit. You may want to have an open-ended holding task for your pupils to get on with if they reach a particular stage faster than their peers. One option is always to give them a short piece of writing (it could even be one of the modelled texts from this book) and ask them to work through the questions at the end of Chapter 1. Or, if it's not considered too radical at the school where you work, perhaps they could simply spend a few minutes reading!

Summary

Planning is vital to writing but a plan is a thought process, not a photocopiable sheet. Planning, generally speaking, should be done backwards. The writer first needs to decide where they're going and then decide how to get there – starting with the ending and the conclusion and then building up the layers of the story until they reach the beginning. Then they are ready to write. However, being ready to write doesn't mean being ready to lay the text out perfectly. On the contrary, a good writer drafts, edits, redrafts and re-edits over and over again. This is a complex skill and we need to model it explicitly for our pupils.

Where next?

So you've researched and planned your piece of writing and you're ready to go. The next question, then, is how to get started with the 'real', 'actual' writing. That is the subject of the next chapter.

Resources and modelled texts

Hero's Journey planning template

We have written the Hero's Journey into more child-friendly terms and created this template for you to use with your pupils. Once again, the written plan should be the very last stage.

Act 1

The hero's imperfect world is introduced.	Percy Jackson keeps getting expelled from schools. Matilda's family are ignorant and unkind. Luke Skywalker is unhappy on his uncle's moisture farm.
The hero is called to adventure.	Harry Potter receives a letter from Hogwarts. Luke sees Princess Leia's message to Obi-Wan Kenobi. Shrek is asked to go on a quest.

The hero rejects (or is refused) the call to adventure.	Lucy tells her siblings about the magic wardrobe, but they don't believe her.
	Bilbo Baggins refuses to leave Bag End.
	Marlin won't ever swim far from home.
The hero meets a mentor.	Harry Potter meets Hagrid.
	Miss Honey encourages Matilda.
	Percy Jackson trains with the other demigods.
The hero crosses the point of no return.	Percy Jackson arrives at Camp Half-Blood.
	Harry Potter leaves the Dursleys with Hagrid.
	Lyra heads north with the Gyptians.
Act 2	
The hero proves their worth.	Percy Jackson defeats the hellhound.
	Lyra helps to rescue an armoured bear.
	The Pevensie children reach Aslan's Table.
The hero grows in strength.	Percy Jackson defeats several monsters, as he and his friends cross America.
	Matilda starts to control her mysterious powers.
The hero almost loses everything.	Obi-Wan Kenobi dies, as Luke and his friends are surrounded by stormtroopers.
	Aslan is murdered and the White Witch raises an army.
	Percy Jackson faces Hades.
Act 3	
The hero is rewarded for surviving the ordeal.	Simba sees his father, reminding him who he is.
	Aslan returns and takes Lucy to the battle.
	Percy Jackson returns from the Underworld.
The hero heads towards the final battle.	Percy Jackson confronts Ares.
	Simba returns to Pride Rock to reclaim the kingdom.
	Luke Skywalker turns off his targeting scanner.
The hero is victorious.	Matilda uses her powers to terrify Miss Trunchbull.
	Percy Jackson heads to Olympus.
	Luke Skywalker destroys the Death Star.
The hero returns home.	Marlin brings Nemo safely home.
	The Pevensies leave Narnia through the wardrobe.
	Percy Jackson returns to his mum.

Modelled writing

Mrs Nethercott

Here is a short story that demonstrates perfectly why planning needs to happen backwards. Only once you know how the story ends can you truly understand the significance of the opening paragraph. It is rich food for discussion with your pupils, although you may need to be sensitive about some of the themes involved.

Mrs Nethercott set her husband's place at the table as she did every evening – with a place mat, a knife and fork and a white china plate. Then she set her children's places. First, she put a plate out for Betty, her eldest daughter, at the seat facing the window. Betty always liked to look out of the window when she was eating so that she could see the red squirrels in the garden. Next, Mrs Nethercott set little George's place. There was no plate for him – he was such a fussy eater and he'd only eat anything if it was served in his special blue bowl with a picture of a train on it. George loved trains.

Mrs Nethercott went back over to the stove and drained the vegetables, which had started to boil over. She mashed the potatoes and took the pork chops out of the oven, serving up her dinner on her own plate. She looked at the clock. This would've been the time that Mr Nethercott would usually come home. Sometimes he'd come in full of joy and energy – with a bunch of flowers that he'd bought for her on the way home. Sometimes he'd have had a bad day and he'd be more gloomy; but he'd always find a smile for her even then.

There'd be no flowers today, of course, nor even a smile. Not anymore. Not since that fateful summer night during the battle for Britain's skies. 'It is with the deepest regret…' That was how the letter had begun. She'd known just from those six words and the RAF letterhead what it would say. Mrs Nethercott carried her solitary plate of food over to the table. She felt a raindrop on her shoulder and looked up at the hole in the ceiling and out to the sky above. She still couldn't bear to get it fixed. The children's bedroom used to be directly above the kitchen. They'd both been in there when the bomb hit.

Mrs Nethercott sat down with her dinner and, as she had done every evening for the last two years, she ate alone.

Chapter 13
Opening ceremony: Writing the first line

No one who lived in the UK in 2012 will ever forget the opening ceremony of the London Olympic Games. We tuned in with a certain amount of scepticism, imagining that we'd be witnessing a parade of silly British stereotypes, perhaps presented by Ant and Dec. Instead, Danny Boyle's masterpiece exploded onto our screens, grabbed the nation (if not the world) by the collar and said, 'watch this'. There was smoke, there were drums, there were pyrotechnics and the sheer number of people involved was utterly spectacular. In the opening segment, vast industrial chimneys rose up through the floor of the Olympic stadium until, eventually, people dressed as ordinary working-class men and women from the early twentieth century were shown toiling and labouring to forge the five Olympic rings. It was big, it was emotional and it was compelling. It sucked us in and demanded that all of us invest in what was to follow. It did exactly what an opening has to do.

Why it matters

Why have we left it until Chapter 13 to talk about openings? Wouldn't this have been the logical place to start the book? Only if you assume that writing the opening must be the first step in the writing process. This is a misguided assumption, and it is what can sometimes lead our pupils to sit staring at a blank page for ten minutes before they get anything written beyond the date. As we discussed in Chapter 12, very often it is useful to fully understand what it is you're introducing before you introduce it. At the time of writing the first draft of this chapter, the introduction to this book was yet to be written. As we write, plans change and themes emerge. This will influence what we want to say at the very beginning.

If our pupils are writing fiction, their opening should foreshadow later developments. This means that they need to know what those future developments are! We all discourage our pupils from using a predictable opening like 'Once upon a time', not just because it's predictable but also because it's not relevant to *that story*. It just tells the reader that they're about to read a story but it hasn't started yet. By comparison, think about the effect of an opening like this:

Have you ever wondered what would happen if you could control your own dreams?

We would all, at the very least, read on to the next sentence, right? An opening line like this is giving the reader a number of messages. It's telling them that their time is not going to be wasted – that we're getting straight to the point. It's also promising that something interesting is going to happen. Perhaps this will literally be a story about someone who learns to control their own dreams, or maybe the opening line is a more abstract introduction to the events of the story. Either way, an opening like this gives the reader confidence that the writer *knows where the story is going*. In order to write a line that inspires this sort of confidence, a writer probably should know exactly where the story is going!

The other important point to make about opening lines is that (as with all lines) there is no such thing as a bad first draft. You can always write something rubbish and come back to sort it out later. Sometimes, this can be a springboard into writing a fantastic story and then, once the story is more or less completed, it becomes easier to think of the right words with which to begin.

How to do it

Don't always start at the beginning

In this chapter, 'when to do it' is at least as important as 'how to do it'. If one of your pupils tells you 'I'm not sure how to start it', tell them to leave a space and write a different part first. In many ways, it can be very beneficial when writing fiction to start with the ending. Then the build-up and revelations that lead the reader there can be 'retrofitted'.

A major problem here is the disconnect that currently exists between the way in which adults write (usually on a computer) and the way that we teach children to write (usually with a pen and paper). This is a conundrum that schools are going to have to resolve in the medium-term future but, until they do, we are going to have to find ways in which to simulate the most significant advantages of word-processing when we ask pupils to write by hand. When it comes to writing stories, this may involve encouraging them to dash off a rudimentary opening that they can come back to later.

As we discussed in Chapter 12, it is important to emphasise to all our pupils that there is no such thing as a bad first draft.

Make an impact

Like the drums and cordite of the 2012 Olympic Opening Ceremony, the start of a story needs to make an impact. It needs to create shock, surprise, sympathy or suspense. The easiest of those for your pupils to manage might be the last one. In Chapter 11, we explored various mechanisms for eliciting feelings from the reader, and we discussed three specific steps that your pupils can tackle to build suspense in their stories. If they can start building that suspense from the very first line, so much the better. Consider the opening of *Mortal Engines* by Philip Reeve (2001):

> **It was a dark, blustery day in spring, and the city of London was chasing a small mining town across the dried-out bed of the old North Sea.**

There is a lot to like about this opening. The very first clause is utterly mundane, telling us what the weather was like, and one might almost be tempted to cry, 'Boring!' It is notable, however, that even in this most unremarkable of clauses, something is amiss. We seldom think of spring days being *dark*. Is this a warning? A foreshadowing of something to come? Furthermore, the *ordinariness* of the opening clause serves to highlight the *strangeness* of the remainder of the sentence. We're familiar with the concept of London, but not with the notion that London could be *chasing* something. Already, we're introduced to the idea that an entire city is on the move. We're then hit with the setting for this peculiar scene: the dried-up bed of the old North Sea. This immediately gets us speculating that we must be in the future, and that something very strange has happened in the time that has elapsed since the present day. We are immediately intrigued and encouraged to keep reading.

Think ahead

When writing *Mortal Engines*, Philip Reeve was inspired by the opening line of George Orwell's *1984* (1949):

It was a bright, cold day in April and the clocks were striking thirteen.

We don't usually think of April days being cold and, of course, clocks don't usually strike 13. The emphasis on time and routine starts to create, from the very beginning, the atmosphere of militaristic rigidity in which the events of the book take place. The number 13 itself is associated with bad luck and misfortune, making the reader unsettled. Good opening lines look ahead, foreshadowing what is to come or deliberately misdirecting the reader.

That is not to say that opening lines have to be dramatic. One of the finest children's books of the past century is surely *When Hitler Stole Pink Rabbit* (1971), Judith Kerr's semi-autobiographical account of a Jewish girl fleeing Nazi Germany with her family. The opening line is simply this:

Anna was walking home from school with Elsbeth, a girl in her class.

You might feel that the impact of this opening line is disappointingly minimal. It is, after all, utterly banal – describing two entirely normal children doing something entirely ordinary. In this case, however, that is precisely the point. A child picking up this book will identify immediately with Anna. The sentence conveys no hint that there is anything unusual about the setting in which she lives or the danger that she faces. There, a young reader will think, is a child *just like me*. This serves to highlight the unspeakable injustice of the persecution that follows.

Summary

The opening of your story has the power to make or break your reader's interest. Good openings command the reader's attention and pull them into the story. Teach your pupils a variety of different techniques for opening their stories, and remember that it is sometimes easier for them to write the introductory paragraph once they know what it is that they are introducing. The beginning can be written at the end.

Where next?

So, you've written an opening line that Dickens himself would be proud of. What next? Well, now the challenge is to keep the momentum going by making connections between your paragraphs and giving your writing a sense of fluency and flow.

Resources and modelled texts

Modelled writing: Linden Hall

All of the extracts in this section are openings of a story called 'Linden Hall'. The characters and setting remain the same for each opening but each is written in a different style. Read them with your class and discuss. Ask your pupils to think about which style of opening they prefer – can they explain why? What techniques has the author used to command the reader's attention from the start? What are the strengths and weaknesses of each style of opening paragraph?

Dialogue starter

This version of the story starts with a conversation between Tammy and Henry. The benefit of this is that the reader gets a sense of what the characters are like and their relationship with one another. The downside is that it can end up with a lot of exposition as the characters 'explain' what is happening to the reader.

'Henry!' Tammy shouted after her younger brother, but he was too high up to hear her. She started to climb the wall.

'Henry, I'm not too sure about this.'

'Don't worry, sis. No one has lived in this house for years. It's totally abandoned – trust me.' Henry reached out his hand and helped Tammy over the stone wall.

'I don't see why we can't just go trick or treating like everybody else. Why, on Halloween, do we have to visit the creepiest house in the neighbourhood!'

'We go trick or treating every year. It's time to mix it up a bit – do something different. You don't want to be like everyone else, do you, sis?'

'Well no, but when I said that, I meant I wanted to wear my own clothes and listen to different types of music – I didn't mean I wanted to trespass in an abandoned house on Halloween!'

She scowled. Henry grinned back. 'Live a little. Follow me!'

Mid-action

This version starts in the middle of the action – Tammy and Henry are climbing the wall to get into the garden of the abandoned house. On the one hand, an opening like this drags the reader straight into the story – there are no introductions, no exposition or explanation. The risk with opening the story like this is that the reader isn't yet invested in these characters, so doesn't really care what happens to them either way. The reader might also lose patience if they don't know what is going on for too long.

> Tammy reached up and grabbed hold of the wall to steady herself. Her brother, Henry, was scaling the wall with ease. She scanned the wall, looking for her next foothold, before carrying on. The stone was cold and hard to grip but she kept going. Reaching up as far as her arm would stretch, she pulled herself up with all her strength. Her knees were grazed and sore from smacking against the wall.
>
> She could hear her heart pounding in her chest – the adrenaline was surging through her body and it wasn't just because of the climb. It was the thought of what awaited them on the other side of the wall. She looked up and saw Henry at the top of the wall. With a heavy sigh, she reached up and carried on the climb.

First person

Generally, we would discourage children from writing stories in the first person, as it limits the narrative to one perspective, and very often that first-person voice ends up being the voice of the child rather than the voice of a character. It can, however, be a useful tool to give the reader an insight into a character's thoughts and feelings, which is what we see in this opening.

> I despaired at Henry sometimes, I really did. As far as brothers went, he had to be the most reckless and impulsive of them all. Like today, I had wanted to go trick or treating but he said he had something else planned. If I had known what his plan was, I would never have agreed to it, but here we were. Well, here I was, at the bottom of the wall, while Henry scampered up it effortlessly.
>
> I reached up, being careful not to put my hand on any of the nettles that were covering the wall. The stone was cold and sharp but I pulled myself upwards and found a nook for my foot. I called after Henry, but he was too far ahead at this point; he was almost at the top of the wall. Sighing heavily, I carried on. I could hear my heart pounding in my chest; I was nervous about what was awaiting us on the other side.

Character-focused

In this version, the focus is on introducing the characters and giving the reader a sense of their personalities. By doing this, the reader is more likely to be invested in what happens to the characters for the rest of the story (if they like them!).

Tammy looked up at her younger brother Henry, confidently scaling the wall without a care in the world. *Why couldn't she be more like that?* she thought to herself. Henry was fearless, confident and bold – it had been his idea to come to the abandoned house on Halloween of all days. He was always doing stuff like this – like the time he suggested they went camping in the middle of the marsh. Tammy had been terrified and had not slept a wink all night, unsettled by the strange noises and haunted by imagined dangers. It's not that Tammy wasn't brave. She would always stand up to bullies at school and was not afraid to speak her mind. She just hated unnecessary risk and would view everything from the perspective of risk and reward. For example, the risks attached to trespassing in this creepy, abandoned house were: risk of injury, risk of arrest, risk of being haunted by demons… she could go on. And the rewards of breaking into a creepy abandoned house? Getting to see inside a creepy, abandoned house. That was it and it didn't seem worth it to Tammy. She groaned in frustration; Henry was at the top of the wall – there would be no convincing him to turn back now. To be honest, there had been no convincing him since he first suggested it last week – once Henry got an idea in his head, it was impossible to get him to change his mind. For a moment, she considered leaving him there. She could easily walk away at this point – he might not even notice. She felt a pang of guilt at the thought – what if he fell and got injured and she wasn't there to help? What if he got scared and she wasn't there to reassure him? With a heavy sigh, she reached up and started to climb the wall.

Setting-focused

In this version of the opening, the focus is entirely on setting the scene. This can be highly effective if your setting is unusual and not somewhere that the reader will have encountered.

The wall alone should have been enough to put them off. The sharp stone was hugged by nettles and moss, the shadow of the house looming over it. The garden was wild and overgrown – hiding all manner of terrors among the weeds. The coiled branches on the trees stretched out with clawing, gnarled fingers. Dark shadows lurked in the still air and an eerie silence echoed around the garden. The heavy iron gates had been rusted by the elements and years of neglect. The house itself was imposing; it towered over the town like a mountain. The windows that remained were filthy, but most had been smashed in, leaving a jagged border of glass around the frame. There was no light and the October mist shrouded it in mystery. It was at this moment that Tammy and her brother Henry clambered over the garden wall and stood gazing up at the mystery that was Linden Hall.

The back story

This version of the opening fills the reader in on how the characters have arrived at this point in the story, providing a bit of information about the characters and the plot. This helps the reader to build up a sense of the story – it also means that the writer can foreshadow future issues or problems that the characters may face.

Tammy and Henry had always loved Halloween. When they were little, their parents would spend October decorating the house with pumpkins, cobwebs and fake spiders. The children would plan their outfits for weeks in advance, piecing them together from what they could find in their parents' wardrobes and what accessories they could buy with their pocket money. Their parents had never agreed with trick or treating, so instead would host a Halloween party and invite all the children in the neighbourhood. Everyone would dress up, they would play party games and Dad would make his famous spooky spaghetti (spaghetti that had been dyed green with food colouring). As they got older, they did their own thing on Halloween – the parties stopped and they would head to friends' houses or local parks to hang out. Until one year when Henry came up with an idea. Tammy had been unsure but she knew Henry – once he got an idea in his head, it was almost impossible to talk him out of it. Which is how they came to find themselves standing among the weeds in the grounds of the abandoned house, Linden Hall.

Foreshadowing

As we discussed earlier in the chapter, foreshadowing often appears at the beginning of the story as a hint to the reader of what is to come. This is the opening chapter of a story called 'Something to fight for' – it is a longer extract and there is a lot that you could use it for. We think that it is a particularly good example of foreshadowing.

Something to fight for – Chapter 1

Have you ever wondered what it feels like to die? We all think about death all the time, whether we notice ourselves doing it or not. If we lived forever we would never have to worry about time. We would have all the time in the world to do all the things we wanted to. We would never have to talk about 'wasting time' or 'saving time' because we would never run out of it. Yet the world is not like that. If we're lucky, we'll get 80 years to do all the things we want to do. Eighty summers, 80 birthdays, 80 Christmases. If we're not so lucky we may have far fewer years than that; if we're really lucky we still won't have many more than a hundred. Nobody knows when they are going to die, and the truth is that it could happen at any moment. A careless driver or an unusual illness could kill me or you this week, even today. Is it surprising that so many people are scared of death? It seems obvious that death is a dark, terrifying thing – the stuff of nightmares. But I'm not afraid of death. You may not believe me, but it's true. I'm going to tell you about the best and the worst year of my life, when I learned that life, however short, is more wonderful and more precious than I had ever imagined. I am going to tell you about John Ball and the rebellion. My name is Lucy Tyler and this is my story.

It begins on the worst day of my life. I didn't see it coming; none of us did.

I was ten years old. It seemed like an ordinary July day and I was having breakfast with my family. Mum and Dad were both social workers. They helped people who were having problems. Sometimes the people were very poor, sometimes they had illnesses and sometimes they were people who couldn't stop doing things that were hurting them, like drinking too much alcohol or taking drugs. My brother Jake was upstairs. He'd been arguing with Dad again the night before. He was 15 and he wanted to be independent. He was fed up with Mum and Dad telling him what to do. Mum and Dad were fed up with Jake behaving in a way that they considered 'irresponsible'. That night, Jake had come home drunk from his friend's house at midnight, after promising Mum he'd be home by ten. He'd drunk more than he could handle, and that was why he spent 20 minutes in the upstairs bathroom. I know because I could hear him. It wasn't a pretty sound. As social workers and concerned parents, Mum and Dad were understandably upset, and Dad started arguing with Jake as soon as he had finished emptying the contents of his stomach into the toilet bowl. It must have been 2.00 am by the time they stopped yelling at each other and I was finally able to get to sleep. The roof was leaking above the landing and Jake had kicked over the bucket that had been catching the rainwater from the summer showers that just wouldn't go away. It had clattered down the stairs and water had gushed out, ruining Dad's case notes from work that had been sitting on a small table halfway down.

So everyone looked pretty tired as they sat around the breakfast table just six hours later. Mum had bags under her eyes. She was reading the *Smithfield Chronicle* as she ate her breakfast, and I don't think her brain had quite woken up yet because she was slowly spooning salt into her coffee. Dad was more alert than me or Mum. He was leafing through holiday brochures.

'I hope holiday brochures don't disappear now that everyone books everything online,' he mused. 'So what do you think? Spain?'

'Nobody uses them anymore anyway, Dad,' I said, 'apart from you.'

Mum shook her head. 'Alan, it's July already! How has it taken us this long to sort out a summer holiday?'

Dad looked at her and shrugged. 'We've just had so much to think about I suppose, what with Jake's mood swings, and trying to get that bloody roof fixed.'

'I know, but…' Mum curled up her lips as she sipped her coffee. 'Is the milk off?'

I shook my head. 'No, Mum. You put salt in it. I did think it was odd.'

Dad laughed. 'Well spotted Lucy! You don't miss a thing, do you?'

Dad's laugh was cut off a moment later, though, and his face became much more serious. We could hear Jake stomping down the stairs. He lumbered straight through the morning room into the kitchen without a word. His face was pale, his hair was flopping around messily and he was still wearing his dressing gown.

'Jake, dear, you're not even dressed yet!' Mum exclaimed. 'You've got to leave for school in ten minutes!'

Jake wandered back in from the kitchen with a large glass of water and slumped heavily in a vacant chair, rolling his eyes at Mum. He didn't even look at Dad.

'Mum, relax. Seriously,' he muttered in a low-pitch drone, 'I'll be there on time. It's only French first thing and I'm not even doing that next year.' Jake was one year away from his GCSEs, and the following year he would only be doing the subjects in which he was taking exams.

'All the more reason to learn as much as possible while you still can,' Mum said. 'Far too many people leave school now without speaking a foreign language.'

Jake grunted, brushing his thick black hair out of his eyes. 'Yeah, well, I'd better get ready.' He got up and stomped back up to his bedroom.

Mum sighed. 'Do you not think you should say something to him, dear?' she asked Dad. 'We don't want him to go off to school without clearing the air.'

Dad nodded wearily. 'Maybe, but what is there to say? He's running late enough as it is… I'll talk to him tonight, smooth things over then. He was very rude to me last night but I said some things I regret.'

'Why has Jake been so moody recently?' I asked.

Dad puffed out his cheeks. 'He's a teenager, Lucy. Most of them are a bit like that.'

'Will I be like that when I'm a teenager?' I asked.

Dad looked at me and smiled. 'No,' he said, 'you're a girl. You'll be a totally different sort of nuisance.'

'Sexist,' I muttered, reaching for the orange juice.

After we'd all had our breakfast, I went upstairs to brush my teeth and fetch my school bag. I grabbed my school jumper, a blue V-neck with the St Peter's crest at the top left, and I was aware of Jake's thudding footsteps as he went reluctantly downstairs and out of the front door. When I went down again, Mum and Dad were busy getting together all the things they needed for work. Dad was looking at the case notes that Jake had spoilt with the water bucket the night before.

'They'll be all right,' Mum said to him with an encouraging smile.

Dad peered up the stairs. 'If we could have got the roof fixed sooner, this wouldn't have happened.'

'Come on,' Mum said and then, looking at me, 'Are you ready, Lucy?'

'Yes I am,' I said. I was unusually excited about going to school today. The summer term was almost over and today was 'moving up day'. We were going to spend an hour with our new teacher in our new classroom, and since I was going into Year 6, the top year, moving up day seemed like a bigger deal than it had in previous years.

We left the house and Dad locked the door.

'Have a good day,' Mum said to me, kissing me on the cheek. She got into the car, started the engine and drove off.

Dad took the train to work, so I would always walk with him as far as the station and then carry on to school on my own. Sometimes, in the winter, I would wish I could get driven to school like some of my friends, even though I knew it was better both for me and for the planet to walk. Today, however, was a beautiful warm sunny day and I felt perfectly happy walking along chatting to Dad.

'How are you feeling about going into Year 6 then?' Dad asked.

'A little nervous,' I replied, 'but we'll have Mr Wallingford, and he's really funny.'

Dad laughed. 'I considered being a primary school teacher once. It seems like the kids think all the male teachers are cool just because there are so few of them compared with all the women! Especially if they're as young as Mr Wallingford.'

'Mr Wallingford isn't young,' I replied. 'He's 25.'

Dad laughed again. 'Goodness me, if 25 is old, I hate to think what that makes me!'

Just before we reached the station, we passed the offices of the *Smithfield Chronicle*. It was a very normal small grey office building and there was usually nothing remarkable about it. Today, however, it was surrounded by people.

'Look,' Dad said, 'the journalists are on strike!'

I couldn't really see what was happening over the fence that ran across the front of the *Chronicle's* offices. Dad lifted me up onto his shoulders so I could see. I could see all around me and, although it felt a little dangerous, I knew Dad would never let me fall.

Some of the people standing in front of the newspaper offices were wearing smart clothes and ties and looked as though they were dressed for work, but others were wearing jeans and T-shirts. There were about 12 of them in all, men and women, all holding wooden banners. I could just make out what some of them said:

FAIR PAY FOR JOURNALISTS!
STAND UP FOR LOCAL NEWSPAPER EMPLOYEES!

'What on Earth is going on?' I asked Dad.

'It looks like the staff at the *Smithfield Chronicle* are on strike,' Dad said, lifting me down from his shoulders with some difficulty. 'Oof! You're a big girl now. I don't know if I'll be able to do that for much longer.'

'I thought going on strike meant you didn't go to work. They're all here.'

Dad nodded. 'They're here but they're not working. Sometimes, when people think they're being treated unfairly at work, they tell their boss that they're not going to work until the problem gets sorted out. That, very simply, is what it means to go on strike. If you own a business, like the *Smithfield Chronicle*, you can't write the newspaper.

You need a huge team of photographers, writers and editors. With no staff, there's no newspaper. So going on strike is a very serious thing to do. These people must be very angry about something.'

'Don't they get in trouble for doing that?' I asked.

'They would have done in the past,' Dad said.

'But not now?'

Dad shook his head. 'Not if they follow the rules. For hundreds of years, people in Britain and around the world have had to fight for their rights. There are a lot of powerful, greedy people in the world who would make slaves of us if we let them. Thousands, perhaps millions, have been killed and imprisoned fighting to give normal people a bit more power over their own lives. Actually, one of the most famous ones had the same name as you.'

I frowned. 'Someone called Lucy Tyler died to give normal people a bit more power over their own lives?'

Dad shook his head and chuckled, adjusting his thin brown hair to hide the slight bald patch at the back. 'He wasn't called Lucy Tyler.'

'He! I should've known,' I said. 'Why is history always full of boys?'

'He was called Wat Tyler,' Dad continued.

'What?'

'Exactly, but spelled W-A-T. That was his first name. It was probably short for Walter. He stood up for the English people against a cruel king in 1381, over six hundred years ago. Normal people who didn't have lots of money were known as 'peasants' back then, and they marched to London, led by Wat Tyler, and demanded fairer treatment by rich people. They called it the Peasants' Revolt.'

'Did they succeed?' I asked.

Dad shrugged. 'It depends what you mean. In the short term, no. As soon as Wat Tyler got close to the King, he was stabbed by the Lord Mayor of London. The King told the crowds of peasants who had come with Wat Tyler that he would give them all the things they wanted – things like fair pay and a shorter working day. But he was lying. Once the crowds had gone home, thinking they'd won, the King broke all the promises he'd made to the peasants. Then he hunted down their leaders and executed them.'

'So Wat Tyler failed?'

Dad shook his head. 'No,' he said, 'I don't think he did. He is still remembered today, not by everyone, but by a lot of people. He left a memory, a story that wouldn't be forgotten. Eventually Wat Tyler's dream would come true, and however tough people find their jobs now, life's a lot easier than it was for peasants back then. I think Wat Tyler is among the people who made that happen. Without him, maybe these people would never have been allowed to go on strike.'

'Why do children never go on strike?' I asked.

'Because you don't work,' Dad said. 'You have to have a job to go on strike.'

'We go to school,' I said. 'That's a bit like a job.'

Dad frowned at me. 'Don't you go getting any ideas, young lady. The best thing to do at school is work hard and behave yourself!'

Unfortunately, I did go getting ideas. Big ones. Not that day. It hadn't become necessary yet. The following year, though, the ideas would keep coming thick and fast. But it would take John Ball to give me the courage to make those ideas real.

Among the striking journalists, I could make out Roy Kinder-Wigley, the editor of the paper. He was a local celebrity in Smithfield; everyone knew him. His father had been a lord or something. He came into school to talk to us about working for a newspaper once in Year 4, and earlier that year he had interviewed me about the dinosaur I made out of vegetables. It won second prize in a competition at the Smithfield Fair. I talked to him for ages, about choosing the right-shaped marrow for the dinosaur's body, about how carefully I'd had to cut the courgettes to make the dinosaur's legs. I told him about how I'd cut an aubergine into small flat triangular pieces and stuck on each one individually to make the dinosaur's back, and about how I cleverly fixed all the pieces together with cocktail sticks, none of which could be seen when you looked at the finished product. Having given him all this information, I was disappointed when all I found in Mr Kinder-Wigley's article about the fair was a photo of me standing beside my vegesaurus and the caption 'Lucy Tyler, aged 9, made a dinosaur out of vegetables'. I always thought I could be a much better journalist than that.

Dad and I carried on along Smithfield High Street. The sun had brought a lot of people out of their houses and even at that time in the morning it was very busy. As we approached the station, I noticed that Dad seemed to be uncomfortable. He was clutching his chest and his face was screwed up.

'Are you OK, Dad?' I asked.

Dad straightened up and the pain disappeared from his face. 'Yes, I'm fine thanks, Lucy,' he said. 'Just a bit of pain in my chest for a moment. I'm sure it's nothing to worry about.'

We reached the station and Dad kissed me goodbye. 'Have a nice day, sweetheart. I hope you have a nice time with Mr Wallingford.'

'Thanks, Dad. Bye!'

I walked off to school and it still felt like a perfectly normal day. That was the last time I saw Dad alive.

Chapter 14

Making connections: Linking sentences and paragraphs

Often, when we pick up a piece of writing one of our pupils has written, we are tempted to say something like 'it doesn't really flow'. It feels bit disjointed – like a list of points, rather than a single text. Usually, this is because of the way in which sentences and paragraphs have been linked. The way that we link ideas together is important and can have a very significant impact on the way in which the writing is received and interpreted by the reader. However beautifully your pupils construct their sentences and choose their vocabulary, their writing still won't feel coherent unless they stitch it all together properly.

Why it matters

Look at this paragraph:

> **It was Tuesday. We went on a school trip. The coach picked us up at 9.30 am. We were going to the Roman fort. The fort was very big. I was in Rayan's mum's group. Our group was taken on a tour around the fort. There was a museum next to the fort. The museum contained some interesting Roman artefacts. We went to the shop. The coach took us back home.**

This paragraph doesn't feel like a paragraph at all. It reads like a disconnected list of facts that might as well have no relationship with one another. You might feel inclined to say something like 'it doesn't *flow*'. A subtle but crucial element in writing is cohesion – a feeling that a paragraph, or even a whole text, is *one thing*. As adult writers, we achieve this using *discourse markers*: little words and phrases that take us from one sentence to the next or one paragraph to the next.

In the past, some of these handy tools have been considered part of a wider family of words known as 'connectives'. In *The Grammar Book*, we made the case for ditching this confusing and excessively general term. In this chapter, we will stick to the language of discourse markers, and consider nine different jobs that they can do.

You can find out more about how grammar influences cohesion on pages 163 and 164 of *The Grammar Book*.

How to do it

Types of discourse marker

In Chapter 3, we explored some of the differences between spoken and written English. We talked about the way in which speech is peppered with phrases like 'well', 'right then' and 'you see'. These are discourse markers – they introduce, clarify or alter the impact of the words that they accompany. Written English tends to contain fewer discourse markers but those that it does contain are very important. We're going to look at nine situations where discourse markers help us to bring cohesion to our writing.

1. Beginning a text or a section of text

Sometimes we want to flag up to the reader that we are setting out the first of several points or we are setting out the first step of a multi-step explanation. This reassures them from the outset that what they are reading has been logically organised:

> **To start with, it is important to understand what we actually mean when we talk about coastal erosion.**

A sentence like the one above does not, perhaps, fill us with excitement about the content of the text, but if we need to learn about coastal erosion, it reassures us that we are going to be moving at a manageable pace and taking a logical route through the information. Other useful discourse markers to begin a text include:

> **firstly, to begin with, at the beginning, in the first instance, first and foremost, for one thing, initially, at the start, primarily, originally**

No doubt you and your pupils can think of others.

2. Adding to and supporting a previous remark

Sometimes we want to add a piece of information that further demonstrates the point that we've just been making or adds an important piece of information to it:

> **In fact, there are several completely different types of coastal erosion, and they're more different than you might think.**

The words 'in fact' link this sentence to the sentence that we used in the previous example. Rather than two completely separate ideas, the discourse marker is highlighting the relationship between them. Other discourse markers that help us add to and support a previous remark include:

> **furthermore, moreover, in addition, then, also, besides, again, indeed**

3. Sequencing information and ideas

These are particularly useful when writing fiction but they're also important in reports, recounts, etc. They are what some teachers call 'time connectives' (grr):

After that, we will look at the most common causes of coastal erosion.

Other sequencing discourse markers include a motley array of prepositions and adverbs:

previously, firstly, secondly, finally, next, recently, immediately, subsequently, after, before, beforehand, meanwhile, during, while, after, later, eventually

4. Exemplifying and illustrating

Sometimes, we need to make it clear that one statement or section of text is there to provide an example or to make it clearer to the reader what you mean:

For example, while most coastal erosion is caused by the sea, it can also be affected by wasting processes on slopes and subsidence on more muddy coasts.

Other discourse markers used for exemplifying and illustrating include:

such as, for instance, as you can see from, illustrated by, demonstrated when, in the case of

5. Comparing and contrasting

An important and useful way to build cohesion in a text is by drawing the reader's attention to similarities and differences between the statements that you are making:

As with (comparing) all geographical phenomena, coastal erosion differs from place to place. Having said that (contrasting), there are some features of the process that are almost universal.

Other discourse markers used for comparing include:

similarly, likewise, just as, equally, in the same way, by the same token

Those used for contrasting include:

but, yet, whereas, despite, alternatively, on the other hand, conversely, having said that, nevertheless, however, notwithstanding

6. Qualifying

Now it gets a little more subtle. Sometimes, we want to identify the fact that one statement is an exception to another or provides conditions under which it is or isn't true:

Except perhaps for longshore drift, few natural phenomena are quite as fascinating as coastal erosion.

Other useful discourse markers in this category are:

apart from, unless, providing, as long as, if, although, albeit, provided that

7. Cause and effect

One of the most important relationships that two statements can have is that of cause and effect, i.e. stating that one is the cause of the other. This can be very important when reading, criticising and producing persuasive writing. A throwaway 'cause and effect' discourse marker can easily allow a highly questionable logical argument to go unnoticed:

> **Due to the lack of attention that coastal erosion gets in the mainstream media, few people realise just how fascinating it is.**

Other cause and effect discourse markers include:

> **because, as a result of, consequently, owing to, thus, therefore, ergo, given that**

An interesting point worth noting here is that it's very easy to *imply* cause and effect with a simple sequencing discourse marker:

> **After a third consecutive year in which membership dropped, the chairman of the National Coastal Erosion Society has been asked to stand down.**

In the sentence above, no direct connection is stated between the two pieces of information, but the reader is left to assume that the former is the cause of the latter.

8. Emphasis

Sometimes, a writer wishes to convey to their reader that a particular point is simply very important – perhaps more important than any other information contained within that part of the text:

> **Primarily, coastal erosion is about stuff falling into the sea.**

Other discourse markers that do a similar job include:

> **above all, in particular, especially, critically, crucially, most importantly, significantly, notably**

9. Concluding and summarising

When we wish to end a text or a section of text, we may wish to highlight the fact that we are now summarising or drawing a conclusion from what has already been said:

> **When all is said and done, coastal erosion is probably the most fascinating topic that anyone could ever hope to learn about.**

Other examples include:

> **finally, to conclude, ultimately, on the whole, overall, in general, to summarise, basically, in short, in the end, when it comes down to it**

Pronouns and cohesion

It's not just discourse markers that enable us to create a sense of 'flow' between sentences. Where either the subject or the object of a sentence can be assumed from the content of previous sentences, we can substitute them for pronouns. This helps to create a subtle sense of cohesion:

> **Our cats, Iorek and Lyra, were named after characters from *Northern Lights* by Philip Pullman. It's been exceptionally hot lately and it's been too hot to stay outdoors for long. They have spent most of the past week lying on the floor of the lounge.**

There are three sentences here and the subject of the last one is 'they'. Even though we haven't mentioned our cats, Iorek and Lyra, since the beginning of the first sentence, the reader is left in no doubt that we are referring to them. This subtly ties the sentences together and makes them feel like one coherent idea.

Repetition and substitution

Look at this section of text:

> **'Welcome to Marwell Park, my Lord,' said Mr Forbes frostily, bowing stiffly.**
> **'Thank you, Forbes,' Lord Cranforth replied, raising an eyebrow at the old butler.**
> **'This way if you please, my Lord,' Mr Forbes added through gritted teeth, gesturing towards the drawing room.**
> **The young aristocrat led on. It seemed that not everyone at Marwell Park was pleased to see him.**

Here you can see two subtle but important cohesive devices at work. Repetition of key words and phrases, especially the names of key characters and places, is essential if a reader is going to be able to follow a story. Children's stories are often difficult to read precisely because they fail to do this – a character or a place is named once and then the reader is left to remember who or what they are. In the passage above, the simple repetition of the name 'Marwell Park' helps to reinforce the name of the location in the reader's mind. At the same time, however, you don't want to repeat proper names so often that they become utterly monotonous. In this example, Mr Forbes is named on the first and third lines but, in the second, he is referred to as 'the old butler'. Lord Cranforth is referred to by name in the second line and then described as 'the young aristocrat' in the final line. This is called substitution and it has the added benefit of reminding the reader of key details about the characters or places without having to pause the action.

Summary

The categories that we have explored in this chapter are by no means an exhaustive list of discourse markers, and there are some very common ones that can quickly and easily express relationships between two sentences. Think about subtle shades of meaning to be found in phrases like *as it happens*, *to be honest* or *all things considered*. As with everything we discuss in this book, it always comes back to the same point. As always, your pupils need to experiment with language and explore the way in which their choices affect the reader.

Where next?

When you're smack bang in the middle of a piece of writing, it can be hard to see a clear way out. You can find yourself losing focus, struggling, and the writing becomes more chaotic as a result. Our next chapter is about how to maintain control and consistency from start to finish.

Resources and modelled texts

Modelled writing

The suffrage campaign

Try sharing this extract with your class, asking them to identify the discourse markers and discuss what purpose they serve.

> The campaign for women's suffrage began in the late 1800s and was led by two key campaign groups: the National Union of Women's Suffrage Societies (NUWSS), who later became known as 'suffragists', and the Women's Social and Political Union (WSPU), who became known as the 'suffragettes'. To begin with, the two groups had campaigned together; however, they were divided over the approaches to campaigning. The suffragists preferred peaceful campaign strategies such as writing to politicians, creating flyers and holding public debates, whereas the suffragettes believed in more militant strategies, which they believed would gain them publicity – for example, chaining themselves to railings, blowing up postboxes and throwing bricks through windows. According to Emmeline Pankhurst, it was 'Deeds, not words' that would have an impact.
>
> Naturally, the actions of the suffragettes gained more attention, although the attention was not always positive and, in some cases, their violent behaviour lost them support. In addition to this, opponents of the suffragettes used their violence as justification for not giving them the vote – how could these women be trusted to make sensible decisions if they were behaving so erratically? On the other hand, public opinion was changing and it is without question that the actions of the suffragettes kept the matter of votes for women on the political agenda. In defence of their militant actions, Christabel Pankhurst wrote: 'If men use explosives and bombs for their own purpose they call it war, and the throwing of a bomb that destroys other people is then described as a glorious and heroic deed. Why should a woman not make use of

the same weapons as men. It is not only war we have declared. We are fighting for a revolution!' (Riddell, 2018)

Eventually, the vote was extended to more men and women in 1918. The extent to which to campaigns for suffrage contributed to this change is often debated, with some believing the contribution of the suffragists and suffragettes to have been vital and others believing that a combination of WWI and pressure mounting from other countries would have led to women being given the vote eventually.

While the actions of the suffragettes may make for uncomfortable reading, we do ourselves no favour by sanitising history. Should we ignore the violent behaviour of the suffragettes and instead just celebrate their achievements? Or, on the other hand, is it the case that if we wish to learn the lessons from the past, we first need to face up to the whole truth of it?

A not-so-special day

Share this extract with your class and ask them to identify what techniques the author has used to create a cohesive story.

By the time Skye woke up, both her parents had already left for work. She'd hoped that they might have left a present or a card on the kitchen table, but all she saw when she went downstairs was the remains of her sister's breakfast and a plate of untouched toast.

'Morning, Skye,' Nadia said sleepily. 'Mum and Dad have already gone. You'd better grab some toast. We need to leave in ten minutes.' She then slumped in one of the chairs at the table, and started scrolling through messages on her phone.

Skye looked at her expectantly for a moment and then, realising that her sister had nothing more to say to her, she started slowly buttering a piece of toast. Surely her whole family couldn't have *forgotten*? Having buttered the toast, she nibbled it in morose silence.

'Was there any post for me this morning?' Skye eventually asked, hoping the question itself might jog Nadia's memory.

Nadia didn't even look up from her phone. 'No, should there be?'

Skye sighed and shook her head. 'Apparently not.'

Ten minutes later, the sisters left the house. Nadia went to the local secondary school by a different route, but just a couple of minutes after the sisters parted ways, Skye ran into her best friend, Ellie. *At least* she'll *remember*, Skye thought to herself.

'Morning Skye!' Ellie called out cheerfully, and Skye eagerly anticipated her friend's next words – but, in the end, they were, 'Have you done your geography homework?'

'My geo… er… yeah,' Skye replied, crestfallen.

As they continued their journey to school, still Ellie said nothing to suggest that she knew this was a special day.

They arrived at school and not a single one of Skye's friends seemed to know either. She wasn't surprised by Dylan (he never remembered that sort of thing) but not even Hannah or Misha acknowledged it. When the bell went, they made their way to registration and Skye looked hopefully at Mr Andreou, her class teacher.

He must have a list of all his pupils' dates of birth, she thought. *Maybe he'll remember.*

'Morning Skye,' he said, cheerfully enough. 'Come in and sit down.' *Come in and sit down? Was that it?!*

All through the day, it was the same story everywhere she went. Not a single teacher and not a single pupil said the two words that she was longing to hear. No one seemed to remember. No one seemed to care. At last, Skye arrived home under a thick, grey cloud. She fumbled in her pocket for her door key and she could feel her eyes starting to glisten as she opened the door.

Chapter 15

Bringing order to chaos: Consistency and control

In the last chapter, we looked at cohesion – at the way in which your pupils can literally sew the sentences and paragraphs of a piece of writing together so that it appears to *flow*. In this chapter, we are looking at a related but subtly different theme: control. What we want to address here is that feeling you get when you pick up a child's writing and you say something like 'it's just a bit *all over the place*' or 'it's interesting and imaginative, but *a bit chaotic*'.

Much of this chaos can be remedied (insofar as we *want* it to be remedied – a little splash of chaos here and there can actually add a bit of colour to a piece of writing) with other prescriptions that we've outlined previously in this book: being succinct, crafting each sentence carefully, choosing the right register and so on. However, there are other, more specific pieces of advice that we can give our pupils that will enable them to make their writing more controlled and more consistent.

Why it matters

A good story *feels like the same story* all the way through. Novels are rarely read in one sitting, and when we pick up a book again, we want to feel that we are re-entering the same story that we were in before, even though the narrative has moved on. Without wishing to sound too corny, one of the great joys of reading is surely its ability to transport us *somewhere else* – into someone else's life or perhaps into another time, another country or even another world. Fantasy and science-fiction writers talk a lot about world-building: making the world in which their stories take place internally consistent and logical. So, for example, the events that take place in *The Lord of the Rings* are impossible and ultimately ridiculous, but if you immerse yourself in the story for long enough, you develop an understanding of how that world works. You get to understand what sorts of beings might be capable of magic and which characters are likely to be allies. The world starts to take on a sort of logic – even if it is a logic that has no bearing beyond the pages of the book.

World-building isn't just a job for fantasy and science-fiction writers. Even a work of gritty realism set in contemporary Britain needs to have a sense of internal consistency – it is essential in order to make a reader 'suspend their disbelief'. When we engage with any work of fiction, we have to engage in a peculiar form of double-think. A novel, a play, a film or a TV drama is basically just a long and incredibly elaborate lie. To enjoy fiction, we momentarily allow ourselves to believe a lie. Inconsistencies in the writing make this harder for us. The writers of soap operas receive countless angry letters and emails every year pointing out continuity errors. These errors (*they've just introduced Bruce's brother, but he said in a previous episode that he was an only child!*) remind us that the story is a fiction, a lie, and they disrupt our ability to enjoy it.

This is not just an issue when it comes to fiction. To appear authoritative and convincing, a non-fiction text must also be internally coherent. The content of the text should usually be presented in a similar way, and relate to a few central themes. If you read something on one page of this book that completely contradicted something else that we'd said, it would undermine your faith in everything we've told you. In a similar way, nothing knocks our faith in politicians more than revelations of hypocrisy. Consistency inspires trust while inconsistency fosters scepticism. Every teacher knows this to be true when it comes to behaviour management. It's also true of writing.

How to do it

Past and present tense

Let's start with a classic problem: consistency of tense. No doubt you come across this sort of thing all too regularly:

> **Kalia's bus arrived in Morley at exactly 4.16 pm. She checked her bag one last time. The bus stops and she gets off. She unfolds the piece of paper with the directions on.**

The first two verbs in this extract (*arrived* and *checked*) are in the past tense. For the final three verbs (*stops, gets* and *unfolds*) the writer has inexplicably switched to the present tense. This is one of the simplest, most common and most jarring ways in which your pupils will shatter the sense of consistency in their writing, and it happens for a very simple reason: it comes back to the differences between the way in which we speak and the way in which we write. When we tell anecdotes informally to people we know, we tend to do so in the present tense:

> **OK, so I'm sitting there, right, and Paul comes up to me. He's got this weird expression on his face and I just know he's going to say something stupid.**

If you pay close attention to the conversations that you have and hear over the next few days, you will be surprised at how firmly we stick to the present tense when speaking informally. It's also true when we're talking about the future:

> **I reckon we get a cab into town, find a nice pub and have a few drinks there. When Hayley and Chris arrive, we go for dinner.**

It's no wonder, then, that children so easily drift back into the present tense when they're writing. They are constantly torn between the habits that they've developed through conversational English and the conventions of storytelling that they've absorbed through reading. The bad news is that we offer no quick fixes or short cuts around this problem. The only solution is to pick it up in their writing and point it out to them.

One suggestion that we would make is that it is best, for the most part, to insist that their stories are written in the past tense. It's tempting to say 'it makes no difference if it's in the past or the present tense, as long as it's consistent'. There are some fiction books written in the present tense and it can serve a useful purpose. For example, the entire *Hunger Games* trilogy is written in the present tense and it probably adds to the constant sense of threat and danger that Suzanne Collins wants to portray. However, this is the exception rather than the rule, and we feel that it's generally best to master the rules before you learn how to break them.

One of the barriers to maintaining the past tense in a story is the constant need for the *conditional mood*. Characters in a good story are always looking ahead – speculating, hoping, worrying about what is to come. This is essential if we want to intrigue the reader and keep them invested in what is happening. However, it creates a surprisingly tricky grammatical issue when writing in the past tense. Look at this sentence:

I decide that I will wait and get the next bus.

Imagine that you wanted to put this in the past tense. Dealing with the verb *decide* is nice and easy – you just stick a 'd' on the end and make it *decided*. But what about *will wait*? If you leave it as it is (*I decided that I will wait and get the next bus*), it sounds as though you still haven't got on that bus even now, at the time at which you're telling the story. The solution is something that we rarely teach explicitly. To express the future hopes, fears, plans and expectations of characters in the past, we have to use the conditional mood:

I decided that I would wait and get the next bus.

Very often, children reach a point like this in their story (usually involving a *will* that needs to be a *would* or a *can* that needs to be a *could*) and they get confused. This is often where things break down and the present tense sneaks back in. Pointing out this little quirk to your pupils will make it much easier for them to maintain the past tense throughout their writing.

First and third person

This issue is closely related to the question of past and present tense and you're probably just as familiar with it. Take a look at this:

Archie wondered whether he should ask his mum for advice.
'Mum, do you think we should always keep secrets for our friends?'
Mum looked concerned. 'Why do you ask?'
'Don't worry,' I said, 'it's not important.'

At the start of this extract, the main character of the story was Archie, referred to in the third person. By the end, the author has switched to the first person, as though they themselves are Archie. When pupils do this, it is probably because they are (somewhat admirably) putting themselves firmly in the shoes of their character and identifying so closely with them that they *become* them in a narrative sense.

As with inconsistency of tense, there are no silver bullets here. All we can do is pick up these inconsistencies in our pupils' writing and then train pupils to spot them themselves, both in their own writing and when they're reviewing the work of their peers.

Recurring themes

Recurring themes are a hallmark of fluent, consistent writing. They are essential in non-fiction writing and also pretty important in fiction. The idea that a story needs to explore a theme can be alien to children, and they will need some help to understand what you mean – firstly by discussing the recurring themes in stories that you read as a class. It sounds very sophisticated but it's actually quite a simple element for them to incorporate into their creative writing. They just need to pick a topic that is relevant to their characters and their plot – it could be something as basic and universal as loss, love, fear or hope. Challenge them to ensure that their characters' thoughts or conversations come round to that topic a few times during their story, ideally in a way that shows the character learning something about that topic or coming to an interesting realisation about it. No doubt it will be a bit clumsy at first but, as with anything, they will get better at it with practice.

Predictable characters

It's great to have unpredictable plots but you actually want your characters to be fairly predictable. When something happens and your reader correctly anticipates how your character will react, then the reader starts to feel like they've got to know that character. They will inevitably feel more empathy for them and feel a greater level of investment in finding out what happens to them. That is not to say that characters should never do anything unpredictable; good stories are full of moments where the villain is redeemed or the traitor reveals themselves. However, these are deliberate acts of misdirection and they usually come later on in the story, after the reader has got to know the character through their (previously) predictable patterns of behaviour. In Chapter 12, we explored the thinking process involved in planning a piece of writing. A big part of this is ensuring that your pupils have really thought out their characters before they write.

Summary

Consistency is key when it comes to holding the reader's attention. In fiction, this can mean building a world with predictable characters and recurring themes. In non-fiction, this means ensuring that your content is both consistent and coherent: consistency inspires trust while inconsistency fosters scepticism. The biggest barrier that your pupils will face is the disjoint between how they speak and the conventions of how they should write. The best way to address this is to (consistently) point it out to them and provide them with lots of examples of how to ensure that their writing is coherent.

Where next?

The next chapter is the last in this book. So it would make sense that the next chapter is about endings.

Resources and modelled texts

Modelled writing – 5P

As we said earlier, there is no quick solution when it comes to ironing out the inconsistencies in your pupils' writing: you just need to keep pointing them out. Use this extract, which is full of inconsistent tenses and switches between the third and first person, to highlight these errors to your pupils. Note how the text starts in the past tense but switches into the present tense. It also starts in the third person but shifts into the first person before Ms Prakash's phone call to Linda. It might seem obvious to us, but when children are focusing so much on the content of their work, things like tense and person can often get confused.

When you are confident that your class understand what is wrong with the extract, challenge them to rewrite it using a consistent tense and viewpoint.

It was the day of the trip and 5P were VERY excited. They are off to the Science Museum to learn about space. Having given out all the high-vis jackets, Ms Prakash starts to take the register, calling out each child's name in her sunny, positive tone.

'Alice?'

There was no reply. The class started looking down the room on the off-chance that Alice was here but just not replying.

'Does anyone know where Alice is?' Ms Prakash asked. Elder raised his hand.

'Miss, I saw her mum this morning dropping off her sister Evie but Alice wasn't with them. Maybe she was ill?'

Ms Prakash nodded and typed something into the computer. It would be a real shame if Alice missed the trip; she has been looking forward to it for months. I picked up the phone and dialled the office.

'Hi Linda? It's Ms Prakash. Please could you call Alice Phillip's Mum and find out if she is coming in today? One of the boys thought she might be unwell. It's our trip today so if she is coming in she needs to be here by 9.30 am.'

'No prob – I'll call them now.'

'Thank you.'

I put the phone down and turned to the rest of the class – they could barely sit still because they are so excited. She could see Aman and Emily comparing the contents of their lunch bag and several them already slyly nibbling the snacks they had brought with them.

'Please don't eat now, Year 5, we have quite a long coach journey to the Science Museum and I don't want you to feel unwell,' she told her class. Reluctantly, a few of them put their snacks back in their bag. Riley and Chloe were looking through the work pack, keen to start filling it in.

Ms Prakash smiled to herself. 5P could be exhausting at times but they were kind and great fun to teach. Although, as she watched Ben try to sneak another handful of crisps into his mouth, she sensed that it is going to be a very long day!

Chapter 16
Happily ever after: Writing an ending or a conclusion

Our journey is nearing its end. We're approaching the point where the words in this book will run out and the relationship that we've had, us as writers and you as our dear reader, will be no more. If you have read the book all the way through, rather than dipping into specific chapters (surely no one would do such a thing!), then, if we've done our job right, you've learned something and feel ever so slightly enriched by the experience. Getting to the end of a book that you've found interesting or enjoyable is a tiny moment of loss – a poignant parting of ways and a subtle reminder of the passage of time. How, then, does the writer acknowledge this moment? How do we bring a piece of writing to a satisfactory conclusion?

Why it matters

Let's start with the classic closing line and consider what it tells us:

And they all lived happily after.

We all acknowledge this as the classic closing line to a story, yet we consider it lazy and unsatisfactory. Both of these perceptions are important.

Firstly, why is it *the* classic ending to a story? Simply, it is the ultimate *resolution*. After recounting a series of events in which, presumably, the characters faced problems and upheavals, we are assured that those problems and upheavals are gone forever – there is no unfinished business. Whatever hopes and fears we adopted on behalf of these characters can safely now be set aside.

So why do we also consider this ending to be lazy and unsatisfactory? Is it the lack of originality? That is certainly part of the answer but is not the whole story. The main problem, of course, is that *no one* lives happily *ever* after. If the characters in a story are to be believable, we must assume that life's everyday challenges continue after the book has finished – that they will continue to chalk up losses and failures as well as gains and successes. Eventually, we must assume that they will die. This may all seem unnecessarily maudlin but it matters. If we have been persuaded to suspend our disbelief and invest in the fate of an author's characters, then we feel robbed if the ending feels implausible. Nothing angers fans of TV shows more than an ending that they consider unsatisfactory. The same is true when we are reading. A good ending provides closure and resolution, tying up the loose ends and answering the questions that kept the reader gripped throughout the story. To be truly satisfying, however, it has to be believable and congruent with everything else that has happened in the story. It also needs to connect emotionally with the reader. If they have enjoyed the book, they are becoming aware of an impending sense of loss as that experience comes to an end. The author needs to signal that they understand and even share that feeling – they need to honour the bond that they've built with their reader over the course of the story, demonstrating ceremony and solemnity at its ending.

Then there is non-fiction. A non-fiction text is usually designed to inform, explain, persuade or some combination of those three. A non-fiction author must use their conclusion to summarise, to remind and to recap. However, this does not need to be a dry and entirely unfeeling affair. The non-fiction author, too, has travelled on a journey with their reader. As non-fiction authors ourselves, we feel that we too have the right to a bit of ceremony when we reach the end of our book. How is this achieved in a way that feels authentic and appropriate to the genre? For a worthy example, we can turn to one of the most famous and important non-fiction books of all time: *On the Origin of Species* by Charles Darwin. Having outlined the theory of evolution via the processes behind natural selection, Darwin ended his book with the following words:

> **There is grandeur in this view of life, with its several powers, having been originally breathed into a few forms or into one; and that, while this planet has gone cycling on according to the fixed law of gravity, from so simple a beginning endless forms most beautiful and most wonderful have been, and are being, evolved.**

The concept of a 'mic drop moment' didn't exist in 1859, but this assuredly is one. Darwin restates the fundamental conclusion of his work, simply and succinctly, but there is also an effort on his part to ensure that his reader feels invigorated and inspired by it. This will be, in part, because Darwin knew that he had a task on his hands to persuade his Victorian audience. Britain was still a deeply Christian country and his discoveries contradicted a literal interpretation of the Bible. The clause 'having been originally breathed into a few forms or into one' seems to be a conscious attempt to leave room for a divine creator in his account of how life evolved on Earth, knowing that to do otherwise would make it impossible for his words to get a fair hearing. The final line is a joyous celebration of the wonders of nature and eloquently expresses just how epic and extraordinary life itself is. It ends, very cleverly, with the key word of the whole book, *evolved*, alone after an embedded clause. It is almost as if the very word has evolved, like humanity itself, from the noise and excitement of the preceding clauses.

How to do it

Fiction

In bringing a resolution to their stories, you might find it helpful to encourage your pupils to consider three strands: plot, characters and themes. All three strands are related, and bringing closure to one can help to bring closure to the other two.

The first and most straightforward strand is the plot. The ending to a good story resolves any mysteries and delivers outcomes on all the various conflicts, dilemmas, romantic entanglements and dastardly schemes that have been introduced. These don't by any means all need to be happy resolutions. A sad ending can be very powerful and a dark, surprising twist can be thrilling. However, questions need answers and the various pieces of plot that have been thrown up into the air all need to land somewhere.

Bringing resolution to a character is about completing their journey – their 'arc' as people sometimes say when discussing TV shows. Ebeneezer Scrooge's arc is resolved when he sees the error of his ways, understands the value of kindness to others and comes to embrace the true meaning of Christmas. Again, however, a character's resolution does not need to be happy or uplifting. In 1984, Winston Smith's arc ends (spoiler alert if you've never read it and would like to) when, at the moment of his death, he finally 'loves Big Brother'. This resolution is utterly hopeless but it represents a logical destination for the character, which is deeply thought-provoking, if troubling, for the reader. At the end of *Hamlet*, every significant character apart from Horatio is dead. The various rivalries at the heart of the play are all rendered irrelevant, as in-fighting in the Danish royal court enables the Norwegian King Fortinbras to come in and take the throne. All who seek revenge succeed in exacting it, but always at the cost of their own life – resolution spelled out in irony, tragedy and blood. Your pupils may not be writing novels like 1984 or plays like *Hamlet*, at least not yet, but they should be planning specific journeys for their characters, with a clear starting point and a deliberate destination.

A character's resolution is inseparable from the key themes of the story. As we discussed in the previous chapter, recurring themes are crucial to good fiction writing, and children should be encouraged to think about the themes of their own stories even in Key Stage 2. If they can express what it is that they want to say to their reader about their theme, they may find that they have a ready-made closing line. It doesn't have to be anything groundbreaking – just a fairly well-trodden bit of wisdom about their chosen theme:

> **Hope is the most powerful weapon there is.**
> **True love can survive anything.**
> **Integrity means doing the right thing, even when no one is watching.**

If your pupils can learn to plan simple stories, with a couple of characters who go on a journey that brings them back to a recurring theme, and then end on a line like the ones above, they'll almost certainly have produced something of which they can be really proud, and it will give them a great springboard to experiment with their writing further as they get older. Writing a good story isn't actually rocket science, but we do need to spell out some of the steps really clearly to our pupils.

Non-fiction

A good conclusion to a piece of non-fiction writing needs to summarise the key points or pithily recap key arguments. Summarising a text is not an easy skill for some children, even when the text is their own. It requires them to deploy all the tools to aid succinctness which we discussed in Chapter 3. A useful principle to convey to your pupils is that, if it had to, their conclusion should be able to stand on its own, i.e. if someone decided to skip to the end and read only the conclusion, they would be able to get the general thrust of your ideas or argument.

However, a satisfactory ending to a work of non-fiction writing isn't just a summary of the rest of the text. It is also an opportunity to provide what speechwriters call a peroration – a climactic final flourish that raises the enthusiasm of the reader and hopefully puts a bit of fire in their belly about the topic being discussed. This is exactly what Darwin did in the ending of *On the Origin of Species*. When writing a conclusion, pupils might want to throw in a few more descriptive flourishes and literary devices, even if the tone of what preceded it was a bit more formal and measured.

Summary

Endings matter. Done well, they lend credibility, gravity and believability to everything that precedes them. Done poorly, they can undo a lot of good work. The precise techniques and registers involved are different for fiction and for non-fiction, but the fundamental principles are the same: the writer must offer inspiration and closure while acknowledging the poignancy of the moment as they part ways with their reader.

Where next?

As always, the resources and modelled texts on the following pages can be shared with your class when teaching endings. Alternatively, you can see us put our money where our mouth is and read our conclusion on page 164.

Resources and modelled texts

A modelled text for an ending is not actually very useful. After all – you can only really judge how effective an ending is when you know what has come before it. What we do advise is making sure that you read entire novels from start to finish as a class – expose your pupils to a variety of endings and let them decide which are fulfilling and which are disappointing.

Modelled writing

Mystery story

To get your pupils practising the skill of writing story endings, we have created this text. It is the opening of a mystery story for your pupils to write their own ending to.

> He stopped outside the door to check that the strange object was still in his pocket. The rain was unrelenting and the intervals between the lightning flashes were getting shorter. He opened the door carefully and quietly so that nobody would hear him, but he needn't have worried – the loudest rumble of thunder yet shook the very timbers

of the building as he stepped inside. The building's interior was dark and cold, but he could hear footsteps above that told him he was not alone in the house. Not good news. He could feel something soft and slimy under his feet but, without any light, he could not see what it was.

As he continued tentatively down the hallway, he checked his right pocket again. The object was still there, still unmoving and still more sinister than this gloomy old house. Beside the object was a battered cigarette lighter. He took it out and struggled to get a spark as his fingers, still wet from the rain outside, slipped on the flint wheel. Eventually, he succeeded in generating a pitiful little flame and he could just make out the outlines of portraits and mirrors on the walls. All were covered in cobwebs. If he hadn't heard the footsteps, he'd have thought no one had been in this house for years. But now the footsteps had stopped. For a moment he wondered whether he'd imagined them. Maybe this was just a deserted old house…

He paused.

He could feel someone's breath on the back of his neck. Without looking around, he became aware that someone had closed the front door behind him. He swallowed hard. He could hear his own heart pounding in his chest.

'This is it,' he said to himself.

Forgetful Bob

Do you remember Forgetful Bob from Chapter 12? We explored the variety of different endings that there could have been to that story. Well, back by popular demand, here is the story of Forgetful Bob written in full. Well, almost full – we've left the ending out so that your pupils can write their own.

Bob was a good man. He worked hard, gave up his seat to people who needed it on the tube and would be the first to lend you an umbrella on a rainy day. He spent his days running the Post Office in the town of Endelham. Bob loved his job. He loved catching up with the regulars and got immense satisfaction out of helping elderly people with their paperwork, banking and general admin. They were always happy to have a chat, which meant that, over the years, his regulars had become his good friends.

At this point, we should probably mention the tiny flaw in Bob's character, the chink in his armour, the fly in the ointment. Bob was forgetful. He was not just slightly absent-minded, but very forgetful. He forgot birthdays, appointments and a variety of social occasions. He even kept a spare pair of house keys locked in the safe, as he had locked himself out of his house on a number of occasions. At work, he had developed a number of systems to ensure that his forgetful nature did not impact his job: he kept numerous lists and asked his employees to put sticky notes up with helpful reminders, e.g. 'Call Mrs Andrews 10.00 am Tuesday'.

These systems worked and, as a result, Bob's regular customers had no idea he was so forgetful. Which is why Mrs Fielder would have thought nothing of asking Bob to water her plants while she was on holiday. Mrs Fielder loved her plants; they were her pride and joy. She could often be found propagating, watering and repotting plants at the weekend, all the while humming happily to herself. Since her three children had grown up and moved out, her plants had become her surrogate children.

'Normally one of my children would water them for me – but we're all going away together, you see. A big family holiday!'

'How wonderful, Mrs Fielder – I would be delighted to take care of your plants.'

'Oh, thank you – are you sure you don't mind? Two weeks is quite a long time.'

'Do not worry – you live so close it will be no bother.'

'You're an angel, Bob. I'll leave you some of those ginger biscuits that you love. Here are the keys – I'll leave watering instructions on the kitchen table.'

'No problem! And it's number 87, right?'

'That's it – 87 Enfield Close. Thanks again, Bob. See you in a fortnight!'

As Mrs Fielder walked away, Bob made a mental note to put the keys with his own in the safe and write down the dates and address as soon as he had the chance. And had the Post Office not suddenly got very busy, he would have done so. Probably.

Conclusion

Since the Mesopotamian civilisations of the fertile crescent developed the first pictorial systems of writing, and the Phoenicians spread their phonetic alphabet across Europe, the Middle East and North Africa, humans have used writing to communicate with one another. Sometimes writing was used to inform, sometimes to warn, to persuade or to entertain. Writing has enabled our species to transmit complex knowledge down through the generations – to transmit the thoughts of long-dead writers to readers thousands of years later. In writing, humanity finds a form of immortality and permanence. That's why a written contract is considered binding in a way that a spoken agreement is not. To write something is to say 'this is real' even if, as with fiction, it isn't strictly *true*. Writing is also a way for us to convey the fact that we ourselves are real, by expressing the thoughts in our minds and the feelings in our hearts – subjective and intangible concepts made concrete and permanent with ink on a page. Perhaps the simplest phrase used in graffiti is 'X was here', where X is the name of the writer. Perhaps, on some level, that phrase encapsulates the purpose of all writing.

Writing is incomplete without a reader and, throughout this book, we have sought to place that simple reality at the heart of everything. We *write* in order that our words be *read*. There is no useful way to measure 'good writing' beyond the likely effect on our intended audience. That means making our writing shorter, not longer, wherever we can. It means crafting sentences that are easier, not harder, to read. It means, more than anything else, teaching writing as an exercise in empathy.

We all try to expose our pupils to excellent examples of writing in the hope that they will pick up, as if by osmosis, the tools and techniques of a skilled writer. Sometimes they will, but sometimes they will need our help to identify and implement those tricks of the trade that we, as adult writers, deploy with little conscious effort. In this book, we have tried to unpick some of those tricks and shine a light on them, in the hope that you will feel empowered to discuss them with your pupils. We give them these tools not to dictate *how* they write, or to put their writing in a box that somehow stifles their creativity. On the contrary, we can – we *must* – give our pupils all the skills that they need to take their thoughts and feelings and give them physical form on the page. We must empower them not just to express themselves, but specifically to express themselves *to their reader*, whether that is the child sitting at the next desk or a distant descendant centuries in the future. Let them reach out to every potential reader in every place and every time to connect, to communicate and to say that 'I was here'.

References

Brown, F. (1948), 'Knock', *Thrilling Wonder Stories*, December 1948.

Burns, R. (1785) 'To a Mouse, on Turning Her Up in Her Nest With the Plough', in *Poems, Chiefly in the Scottish Dialect* (or *The Kilmarnock Edition*). Kilmarnock: John Wilson.

Campbell, J. (1949), *The Hero with a Thousand Faces*. New Jersey: Bollingen Foundation.

Churchill, W. (1940), 'We shall fight on the beaches', 4 June 1940, House of Commons.

Churchill, W. (1940), 'This was their finest hour', 18 June 1940, House of Commons.

Darwin, C. (1859), *On the Origin of Species*. London: John Murray.

Dickens, C. (1843), *A Christmas Carol*. London: Chapman & Hall.

Gibbons, Aidan (no date), *The Piano Short Animation*. Available at: https://www.youtube.com/watch?v=vNJQagEhvMA

Hail, Caesar! (2016), directed by Joel and Ethan Coen [film]. Working Title Films.

Jennings, A. (2019), *Vocabulary Ninja: Activities to unlock a world of words*. London: Bloomsbury Education.

Kerr, J. (1971), *When Hitler Stole Pink Rabbit*. London: HarperCollins.

Ness, P. (2011), *A Monster Calls*. London: Walker Books.

Noyes, A. (1906), 'The Highwayman', *Blackwood's Magazine*, August 1906.

Orwell, G. (1949), *1984*. London: Secker & Warburg.

Paramour, Z. and T. (2020), *The Grammar Book*. Bloomsbury Education.

Quigley, A. (2018), *Closing the Vocabulary Gap*. Oxfordshire: Routledge.

Reeve, P. (2001), *Mortal Engines*. London: Scholastic.

Riddell, F. (2018), *Suffragettes, violence and militancy*, British Library. Available at: https://www.bl.uk/votes-for-women/articles/suffragettes-violence-and-militancy

Shadowlands (1993), directed by Richard Attenborough [film]. United International Pictures.

Shaw, G. B. (1913), *Pygmalian* [play].

The Morecambe and Wise Christmas Show (1971), BBC.

'The One in Massapequa' (2002), *Friends*, Series 8, episode 18. NBC.

Vebber, D. (2011) 'The Book Job Transcript', *The Simpsons*. Series 23, episode 6. Fox.

Wyatt, D. (2017), 'Roald Dahl letter warning student to "eschew beastly adjectives" goes viral 35 years later'. Independent, 13 September 2017. Available at: www.independent.co.uk/arts-entertainment/books/news/roald-dahl-letter-warning-student-to-eschew-beastly-adjectives-rediscovered-after-35-years-10003181.html

Yellowlees-Douglas, J. (2015), *The Reader's Brain: How neuroscience can make you a better writer*. Cambridge University Press.

Index